英語で日本の
しきたりと文化を
伝える本

Japanese Customs and Culture in English

おもてなし接客英会話
プロフェッショナル
荒井弥栄 著
Yae Arai

二見書房

＊ はじめに

日本を訪れた多くの外国人や、海外で日本に興味のある外国人の方々と接し、すばらしい日本の文化を伝えることも、大事な「おもてなし」だと感じています。この本では、さまざまな日本の文化やマナーを、イラストとともにわかりやすく説明しています。ぜひ、この本をご活用くださり、外国人と素敵なコミュニケーションを取っていただけたらと思います。

おもてなし接客英会話プロフェッショナル
荒井弥栄

✻ Introduction

Each country has its respective cultures and customs. I think that sharing our cultures with each other is how we come to know each other. Japan has a diversity of traditional customs that we can enjoy. I wrote simple-explanations about a lot of Japanese cultures and manners and accompanied them with illustrations in this book. I am very grateful for this opportunity to share our country with you through this book.
Thank you.

Hospitality English Professional
Yae Arai

✽ CONTENTS もくじ

はじめに ……………………………………… 2
Introduction ………………………………… 3
✽本書の使い方 ……………………………… 8

1 Dining manners
食事のマナー

Chopsticks　箸	10
The Basics of Japanese Food　日本食の基本	12
Sushi　寿司	14
Conveyor Belt Sushi　回転寿司	16
Soba and Udon　そば・うどん	18
Tempura　天ぷら	20
Hot Pot Dishes　鍋料理	22
What's Kaiseki-ryori?　会席料理・懐石料理	24
Japanese-style Bar　居酒屋	26
Japanese Sake and Syochu　日本酒・焼酎	28
Ramen　ラーメン	30
Home-cooked Meals　家庭料理	32
Ekiben, Box lunch, and Onigiri　駅弁・弁当・おにぎり	34
Japanese Confectionery　和菓子	36
Japanese Tea　日本茶	38

2 Manners for staying and visiting
宿泊・訪問のマナー

Japanese-style Hotels (Ryokan)　日本旅館	40
Hot Springs　温泉	42
Public Baths　銭湯	44
Shukubos　宿坊	46

Japanese Houses　日本の家	48
Visiting Someone's House　訪問	50
Hospitality Gifts　手土産	52

3　Manners for worshipping and sightseeing
参拝・観光のマナー

Shrines　神社	54
Worship at a Shinto Shrine　神社の参拝	56
Sacred lots and Charms　おみくじ・お守り	58
Temples　お寺	60
Worship at a Temple　お寺の参拝	62
Buddhist Statues　仏像	64
Zazen　坐禅	66
Shakyo　写経	68
Japanese Gardens　日本庭園	70
Castles　城	72
Festivals　祭り	74
Cherry Blossom Viewing Parties　花見	76

4　Experience Japanese customs
日本文化にふれる

Kabuki　歌舞伎	78
Noh　能	80
Kagura　神楽	82
Gagaku　雅楽	83
Bunraku　文楽	84
Kimonos　着物	86

Yukatas 浴衣	88
Sado 茶道	90
Kado 華道	92
Shodo 書道	94
Haikus 俳句	95
Ukiyoe 浮世絵	96
Bonsai 盆栽	98
Shikki 漆器	100
Tojiki 陶磁器	101
Sumo Wrestling 相撲	102
Martial Arts 武道	104
Samurais (warriors) 侍	106
Ninjas (spies in medieval times in Japan) 忍者	107
Origami (the Art of Paper Folding) 折り紙	108

5 Buying souvenirs
お土産を買う

Japanese Souvenirs ① 日本のお土産 ①	110
Japanese Souvenirs ② 日本のお土産 ②	112
Japanese Souvenirs ③ 日本のお土産 ③	114

6 Traditional customs in Japan
日本のしきたり

Annual Events in the Spring　年中行事―春	116
Annual Events in the Summer　年中行事―夏	118
Annual Events in the Autumn　年中行事―秋	120
Annual Events in the Winter　年中行事―冬	122
The New Year　お正月	124
Shinzenkekkonshiki (Shinto-style Wedding)　神前結婚式	126
Ososhiki Funerals　お葬式	128

7 Hospitality English Professional
おもてなし英語フレーズ集

Greetings　挨拶をする	130
Meeting Someone　知り合う	132
Introducing Yourself　自己紹介をする	134
Showing Someone the way ①　道案内をする ①	136
Showing Someone the way ②　道案内をする ②	138
Offering Assistance　手伝いを申し出る	140
Calling　電話をする	142
Caring about Someone　気遣う	144
Welcoming Someone, Asking Someone Something, Chiming in　出迎え・お願い・あいづち	146
Having a Meal　食事をする	148
Advice for Buying Souvenirs　お土産のアドバイス	150
Emergencies　緊急事態	151

＊本書の使い方

本書は、外国の方に日本の文化やマナー、しきたりなどを英語で説明したいとき、また外国の方が日本のことを知りたいときに役立つように作っています。

章タイトルの英語です。

見開き（2ページ）に、1テーマが基本です。

日本語の読みを、ローマ字で記しています。

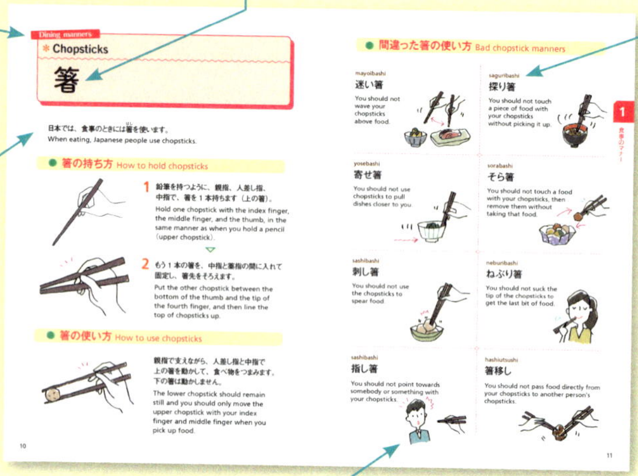

Dining manners
＊Chopsticks
箸

日本では、食事のときには箸(はし)を使います。
When eating, Japanese people use chopsticks.

● 箸の持ち方 How to hold chopsticks

1 鉛筆を持つように、親指、人差し指、中指で、箸を1本持ちます（上の箸）。
Hold one chopstick with the index finger, the middle finger, and the thumb, in the same manner as when you hold a pencil (upper chopstick).

2 もう1本の箸を、中指と薬指の間に入れて固定し、箸先をそろえます。
Put the other chopstick between the bottom of the thumb and the tip of the fourth finger, and then line the top of chopsticks up.

● 箸の使い方 How to use chopsticks

親指で支えながら、人差し指と中指で上の箸を動かして、食べ物をつまみます。下の箸は動かしません。
The lower chopstick should remain still and you should only move the upper chopstick with your index finger and middle finger when you pick up food.

10

● 間違った箸の使い方 Bad chopstick manners

mayoibashi
迷い箸
You should not wave your chopsticks above food.

saguribashi
探り箸
You should not touch a piece of food with your chopsticks without picking it up.

yosebashi
寄せ箸
You should not use chopsticks to pull dishes closer to you.

sorabashi
そら箸
You should not touch a food with your chopsticks, then remove them without taking that food.

sashibashi
刺し箸
You should not use the chopsticks to spear food.

neburibashi
ねぶり箸
You should not suck the tip of the chopsticks to get the last bit of food.

sashibashi
指し箸
You should not point towards somebody or something with your chopsticks.

hashiutsushi
箸移し
You should not pass food directly from your chopsticks to another person's chopsticks.

1 食事のマナー

11

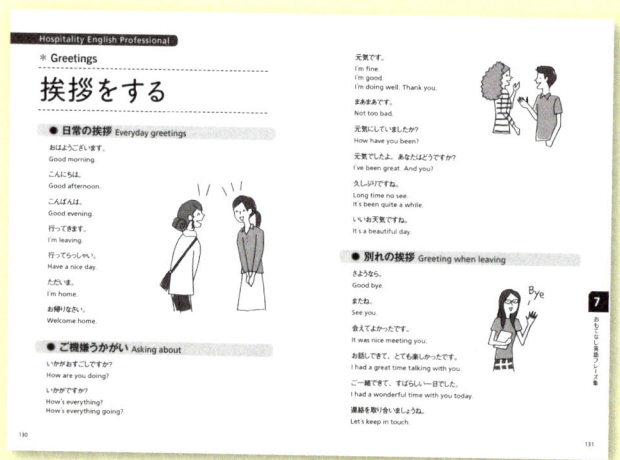

それぞれのテーマの概要を、簡単に説明しています。

イラストを多用し、内容がひと目でわかります。

Hospitality English Professional
＊Greetings
挨拶をする

● 日常の挨拶 Everyday greetings

おはようございます。
Good morning.

こんにちは。
Good afternoon.

こんばんは。
Good evening.

行ってきます。
I'm leaving.

行ってらっしゃい。
Have a nice day.

ただいま。
I'm home.

お帰りなさい。
Welcome home.

● ご機嫌うかがい Asking about

いかがおすごしですか？
How are you doing?

いかがですか？
How's everything?
How's everything going?

130

元気です。
I'm fine.
I'm good.
I'm doing well. Thank you.

まあまあです。
Not too bad.

元気にしていましたか？
How have you been?

元気でしたよ。あなたはどうですか？
I've been great. And you?

久しぶりですね。
Long time no see.
It's been quite a while.

いいお天気ですね。
It's a beautiful day.

● 別れの挨拶 Greeting when leaving

さようなら。
Good bye.

またね。
See you.

会えてよかったです。
It was nice meeting you.

お話しできて、とても楽しかったです。
I had a great time talking with you.

ご一緒できて、すばらしい一日でした。
I had a wonderful time with you today.

連絡を取り合いましょうね。
Let's keep in touch.

7 おもてなし英語フレーズ集

131

7章は「おもてなし英語フレーズ集」です。外国の方との会話でよく使われるフレーズを厳選しています。

イラストで解る！
英語で日本のしきたりと文化を伝える本
Japanese Customs and Culture in English

Dining manners

* Chopsticks

箸

日本では、食事のときには箸(はし)を使います。
When eating, Japanese people use chopsticks.

● 箸の持ち方 How to hold chopsticks

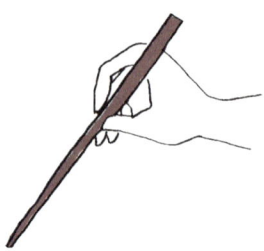

1 鉛筆を持つように、親指、人差し指、中指で、箸を1本持ちます（上の箸）。

Hold one chopstick with the index finger, the middle finger, and the thumb, in the same manner as when you hold a pencil (upper chopstick).

▽

2 もう1本の箸を、中指と薬指の間に入れて固定し、箸先をそろえます。

Put the other chopstick between the bottom of the thumb and the tip of the fourth finger, and then line the top of chopsticks up.

● 箸の使い方 How to use chopsticks

親指で支えながら、人差し指と中指で上の箸を動かして、食べ物をつまみます。下の箸は動かしません。

The lower chopstick should remain still and you should only move the upper chopstick with your index finger and middle finger when you pick up food.

● 間違った箸の使い方 Bad chopstick manners

mayoibashi
迷い箸
You should not wave your chopsticks above food.

saguribashi
探り箸
You should not touch a piece of food with your chopsticks without picking it up.

yosebashi
寄せ箸
You should not use chopsticks to pull dishes closer to you.

sorabashi
そら箸
You should not touch a food with your chopsticks, then remove them without taking that food.

sashibashi
刺し箸
You should not use the chopsticks to spear food.

neburibashi
ねぶり箸
You should not suck the tip of the chopsticks to get the last bit of food.

sashibashi
指し箸
You should not point towards somebody or something with your chopsticks.

hashiutsushi
箸移し
You should not pass food directly from your chopsticks to another person's chopsticks.

Dining manners
✱ The Basics of Japanese Food
日本食の基本

昔ながらの日本食は「一汁三菜(いちじゅうさんさい)」が基本です。
The traditional meal consisting of three dishes and soup is a basic Japanese meal.

一汁三菜は、ご飯、汁物、おかず3品（主菜1品、副菜2品）で構成された、バランスのいい食事です。
Ichiju-sansai consists of a bowl of boiled rice (or other boiled grain), a shiru-mono dish (soup dish), and three side dishes (one main side dish and two sub-side dishes).

● 配膳の位置 Table setting (from guest perspective)

fukusai (nimono)
副菜（煮物）
boiled dishes

shusai (yakimono, sashimi)
主菜（焼き物・刺身）
main dish

fukufukusai (aemono, tsukemono)
副副菜（和え物・漬物）
side dish

gohan
ご飯
rice

shirumono
汁物
soup

● 食事のマナー Dining manners

茶碗、お椀は手に持って食べます。
You should hold your rice bowl or miso soup bowl when you eat.

同じものばかりを集中して食べないこと。
You should not eat same dish repeatedly. Try to finish the different dishes evenly.

大きなものは器の中で、箸で切ります。
You should cut the food smaller on the dish with your chopsticks when there are big pieces.

魚は左から食べること。
You should eat fish from the left.

ご飯にしょうゆやソースをかけないこと。
You should not pour sauce or soy sauce on rice.

ふたつきのお椀の場合、食べ終わったらふたを元に戻します。
When you have a bowl with a lid, place the lid back on the bowl after finishing.

Dining manners

* Sushi

寿司

寿司には、握りずし、巻きずし、ちらしずし、押しずしなどがあります。
There are a few kinds of sushi, for example nigiri-zushi, maki-zushi, oshizushi, and so on.

握りずしは、ひと口大の酢めしに、薄く切った生の魚などをのせたものです。
Putting raw fish slices or shellfish on top of small vinegared rice balls is called "nigiri-zushi".

● **寿司のマナー** Manners for eating sushi

手や箸を使います。
You can use your fingers or chopsticks.

しょうゆは、タネに少しつけます。
For nigiri-sushi, dip the tane (fish) in soy sauce a little.

ひと口で食べましょう。
You should eat it in one bite.

お茶やしょうがは、口の中をさっぱりさせるため、合い間にいただきます。
Green tea and pickled ginger make our mouth freshen up, so we have them when we eat sushi.

● 寿司の種類 Kinds of sushi

toro
とろ
fatty tuna

maguro
まぐろ
tuna

samon
サーモン
salmon

hamachi
はまち
young yellowtail

anago
あなご
conger eel

kohada
こはだ
spotted shad

uni
うに
sea urchin

ikura
いくら
salmon roe

hotate
ほたて
scallop

akagai
あかがい
ark shell

ebi
えび
shrimp

ika
いか
squid

tekkamaki
鉄火巻き
tuna sushi roll

tamago
たまご
sweet egg omelette

刺身とは？ What's sashimi?

刺身は、まぐろ、鯛、いかなどの新鮮な魚介類を、生のまま薄く切った料理です。

Sashimi is a dish consisting of thinly sliced raw tuna, sea bream, cuttlefish, or other fresh fish or shellfish.

わさびといっしょに、しょうゆにつけて食べます。

People dip it in soy sauce and eat it with wasabi (green horseradish paste).

Dining manners

✲ Conveyor Belt Sushi

回転寿司

回転寿司は、ベルトコンベアに乗って回っている寿司を
自分で取って食べる、安価な寿司店です。
This restaurant is the place where you pick sushi from a rotating conveyor belt. They are easy on the wallet.

回っていない寿司を注文することもできます。
If the belt doesn't have what you want, you can make a special order as well.

お茶は自分で用意します。粉末茶などを湯のみに入れて、お湯を注ぎます。
You have to prepare tea by yourself. Put the green tea powder in the tea cup and pour hot water in your cup.

食後に、食べた皿の枚数を数えて精算します。
Wait for the server to count the plates first, then go to the cashier.

回転寿司のマナー
Manners of conveyor belt sushi

寿司だけ取らずに、皿ごと取りましょう。
Don't just take the sushi, take the entire dish.

一度取った皿を、戻すのはやめましょう。
If you pull a plate off the line, you can't put it back.

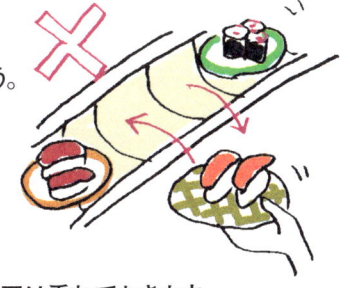

食べたあとの皿は重ねておきます。
You should pile up the dishes when you finish eating.

寿司の作り方 How to make sushi

1 炊きたてのご飯に、調味した酢を入れて混ぜ、うちわなどで冷ます。
Mix just-cooked steamed rice and sushi vinegar, then fan to cool it.

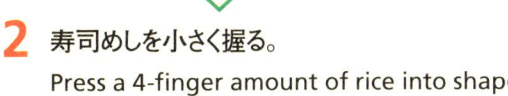

▽

2 寿司めしを小さく握る。
Press a 4-finger amount of rice into shape.

▽

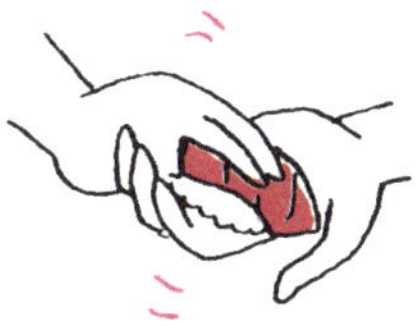

3 寿司めしの上に、タネをのせて握る。
Put vinegared rice on neta and make nigiri-zushi.

Dining manners
✳ Soba and Udon
そば・うどん

そばの原料はそば粉で、つなぎに小麦粉や山いもを使います。茶色で細く、少しかたい食感です。

Soba is brownish noodle made from buckwheat flour. Wheat flour and yam are also used in the binding agent. It is thin and a little hard.

うどんの原料は小麦粉で、白くて太く、やわらかい食感です。
Udon is a white noodle made from wheat flour. It is thick and soft.

● そば・うどんのマナー
Manners for eating soba or udon

音をたてて食べます。特に熱いそばやうどんは、音をたてて食べると温度が下がり、やけどしません。

You can make noise when eating these noodles. Slurping when you eat hot soba or udon helps prevent you from burning your tongue.

ざるやもりは、そばちょこを持ち上げて食べましょう。

When you eat Zaru-soba or Mori-soba, you should raise the soba-choko (a cup used to hold the soup that accompanies Japanese buckwheat noodles).

● そば湯 Soba-yu

ざるやもりには、そば湯がつきます。食べ終えたら、そばつゆに、そば湯を加えて飲みます。

Zaru-soba and Mori-soba come with Soba-yu (hot buckwheat water). You can drink the mixture of soba-tsuyu and soba-yu after eating the noodles.

sobayu
そば湯
hot buchwheat water

sobatsuyu
そばつゆ
soba dipping sauce

sobachoko
そばちょこ
sobachoko

● 主なメニュー The main items on menu

zaru
ざる
cold soba noodles topped with sliced dried seaweed served on a bamboo draining basket with dipping sauce

mori
もり
chilled soba served on a wicker basket or in a shallow steaming basket with dipping sauce

kake
かけ
soba in hot broth

kitsune
きつね
udon with deep-fried tofu

tanuki
たぬき
noodles with bits of deep-fried tempura batter

tempura
天ぷら
deep-fried fish and vegetables noodles with tempura

tsukimi
月見
udon noodles in soup, topped with an egg

kare
カレー
thick Japanese wheat noodles with curry soup

kamonamban
鴨南蛮
noodles with duck meat and welsh onions

Dining manners

✱ Tempura

天ぷら

天ぷらとは、野菜や魚介などに衣をつけて、揚げたものです。
Tempura include vegetables and seafood that have been dipped in batter and deep-fried

● 天ぷらのマナー Manners for eating tempura

天ぷら専門店のカウンターでは、揚げたての天ぷらが、ひとつずつ出されます。
Tempura is served one by one at a counter seat of a tempura specialty restaurant.

揚げたてを、天つゆか塩をつけて、すぐに食べます。
You should eat tempura with salt or thin dipping sauce right after being served.

天つゆには、大根おろしやしょうがを入れます。
Put grated daikon radish or ginger into the thin dipping sauce for tempura.

天ぷらの盛り合わせ
assorted tempura dish

盛り合わせでは、淡白な味のものが手前に、濃い味のものが奥にあるので、手前から順番に食べます。
There are bland-tasting pieces on the front side of the assorted tempura dish and, strong-tasting foods in the back. You should start eating from the front.

● 天ぷらの種類 Kinds of tempura

ebi
えび
shrimp

kisu
きす
Japanese whiting

anago
穴子
conger

ika
いか
squid
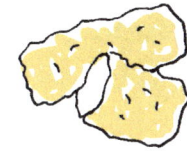

kabocha
かぼちゃ
pumpkin

shishito
ししとう
a variety of green pepper.

nasu
なす
eggplant

maitake
まいたけ
hen-of-the-woods

天ぷらの作り方 How to make tempura

1 卵、冷水、小麦粉を混ぜて衣を作る。
You can make batter by mixing egg, cold water, and wheat flour.

▽

2 野菜や魚介に衣をつけて、約180℃の油で揚げる。
Dip the fish and vegetables into the batter and deep-fry at 180°C.

▽

3 油をよくきって、器に盛る。
Drain the oil and serve the tempura on the dish.

Dining manners

✱ Hot Pot Dishes

鍋料理

寒い時期になると、温かい鍋料理を食べる機会が増えます。
We have many chances to eat hot pot dishes during cold winters.

食卓に、大きい鍋と卓上コンロがセットされ、そこで魚介や肉、野菜などを調理したり、温めながら食べます。
Put a pot over a burner in the center of the table and boil vegetables, seafood, meat, and other ingredients.

● 鍋料理のマナー Manners for eating hot pot diches

菜箸やお玉を使います。
Use the meal serving chopsticks and a ladle.

自分が食べる分だけ、取ります。
Dish out only the amount food that you can eat.

鍋の中を、箸で混ぜすぎないように！
Don't overmix the food in the pot.

主な鍋料理 Main hot pot dishes

yosenabe
寄せ鍋

Boiled vegetables and other ingredients are served in soup seasoned with soy sauce, miso, salt, sake and so on.

shabushabu
しゃぶしゃぶ

The ingredients such as thinly sliced beef and vegetables are quickly boiled in kelp-based broth in a shallow pan and then eaten after being dipped in a sauce with some condiments.

mizutaki
水炊き

Chopped chicken, tofu, and vegetables are boiled in stock and then eaten with citrus juice and soy sauce.

sukiyaki
すき焼き

Sliced beef, vegetables, and bean curd are cooked in a pan on the table with soy sauce, sugar, and sake added for flavoring.

chankonabe
ちゃんこ鍋

These hot pot dishes are eaten mainly by professional sumo wrestlers in Japan.

motsunabe
もつ鍋

This is a hot pot stew made with offal, vegetables, and often miso.

Dining manners
*What's Kaiseki-ryori?
会席料理・懐石料理

● 会席料理とは What's kaiseki-ryori (banquet style)?

会席料理は、宴席などで出される正統な日本料理の形式です。

Kaiseki-ryori is a traditional Japanese-style meal served at banquets.

現在では、高級な日本旅館や料亭などで多く供されています。

It is mainly served at the high class restaurants and at Japanese-style hotels.

● 懐石料理とは What is Kaiseki-ryori (tea ceremony style)?

懐石料理は、もともとは、茶道でお茶をのむ前に供される軽い料理です。

Kaiseki-ryori was originally served in small portions during the traditional tea ceremony.

会席＝懐石料理と区別して、「茶懐石」とも呼ばれます。

Kaiseki-ryori is sometimes called "chakaiseki."

● 供される順番 Order of serving

会席料理は、次のような順番で料理が出てきます。
（普通の日本旅館などでは簡略化され、全部一緒に出てきます。）
Dishes are served one after another in kaiseki-ryori.
(They are all on a tray and are served in most Japanese hotel.)

食事のマナー 1

1 先附（前菜） sakizuke (zensai)
appetizers

2 八寸 hassun
An appetizer made of ingredients from the sea or mountains.

3 椀 wammono
wooden ball

4 向付（お造り） mukozuke (otsukuri)
Mixed Sashimi Platter

5 強肴（煮物） shiizakana (nimono)
simmered food

6 鉢肴（焼き物） hachizakana (yakimono)
broiled fish

7 揚げ物 agemono
deep-fried food

8 蒸し物 mushimono
steamed food

9 止め肴（酢の物） tomezakana (sunomono)
vinegared food

10 ご飯・止め椀・香の物 gohan・tomewan・konomono
rice, miso soup, pickles

11 果物（水菓子） kudamono (mizugashi)
fruits

※組み合わせ、順番は、店によって多少違いがあります。

The combination and order differ slightly at each restaurant.

Dining manners
* Japanese-style Bar
居酒屋

居酒屋では、お酒を中心として、つまみや簡単な料理が楽しめます。
You can enjoy alcoholic drinks with a light meal.

ビール、日本酒、チューハイ、ワインなど、さまざまなお酒がそろっています。
There are beer, Japanese sake, shochu highballs, wine, and so on.

● ビールの注ぎ方・注がれ方
How to pour and being poured beer

注ぐときは、ラベルを上にして、下に手を添えます。
When you pour beer into someone's beer glass, you should hold the bottle of beer with the label side up.

注がれるときは、グラスを両手でまっすぐ持ちます。
When someone pours beer into your glass, you should hold the glass with both hands.

● お通し Amuse bouche

多くの居酒屋では、注文しなくても最初に小鉢が供され、その分の料金を取られます。
In an izakaya, they start by serving you a small bowl of something to eat without you ordering it. They will charge you for it.

人気のつまみ Popular dishes

edamame
枝豆
boiled soybean

hiyayakko
冷奴
chilled tofu

tsukemono
漬け物
pickles

yakitori
焼き鳥
char-broiled chicken

motsuni
もつ煮
simmered pork innards / innards stew

ika-no-shiokara
いかの塩辛
salted squid

tori-no-karaage
鳥のから揚げ
fried chicken

korokke
コロッケ
croquette

hokkeyaki
ほっけ焼き
broiled hokke fish

Dining manners

✻ Japanese Sake and Shochu

日本酒・焼酎

日本酒は、米と麴（こうじ）と水でつくられた「醸造酒」です。甘口と辛口があります。

Japanese sake is fermented liquor which is made from rice and malted rice and water. It has a dry taste and a sweet taste.

原料や精米歩合によって、吟醸酒（ぎんじょうしゅ）、純米酒、本醸造酒などに分けられます。

Japanese sake is divided into gInjoshu, junmaishu and honjozoshu according to the ingredients and the ratio indicating the quality of polished rice gained from the quantity of brown rice.

焼酎は、日本の代表的な「蒸留酒」です。

Shochu is a Japanese representative liquor of Japan.

🟢 日本酒の注ぎ方・注がれ方
How to pour and how to hold the glass when being poured

注ぐときは、相手がおちょこを持ったら、とっくりから八分目まで注ぎます。

When someone holds a small sake cup, you pour the Japanese sake to fill eight-tenths of a sake cup from the sake decanter.

注がれるときは、おちょこを右手に持ち、下に左手を添えます。

When someone is pouring Japanese sake for you, hold the sake cup with one of your hands and touch the bottom of the cup with your other one.

ochoko
おちょこ
sake cup

tokkuri
とっくり
sake decanter

● 日本酒の飲み方 How to drink Japanese sake

日本酒は、温めても冷やしてもおいしく飲むことができます。温度の違いで、それぞれ呼び名があります。

You can enjoy both cold sake and hot sake. Both of them are so named because of the difference of the temperature.

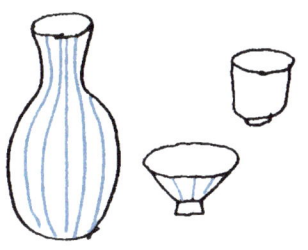

冷酒（冷やした酒）
Reishu (cold sake)

冷や（常温）
Hiya (ordinary temperature)

人肌燗（35℃程度）
Hitohadakan
(at about 35 degrees Celsius)

ぬる燗（40℃程度）
Nurukan
(at about 40 degrees Celsius)

熱燗（50℃程度）
Atsukan
(at about 50 degrees Celsius)

● 焼酎の飲み方 How to drink shochu

焼酎は使われる原料によって、麦焼酎、いも焼酎、米焼酎などに分けられます。

They are divided into mugi-jochu, imo-jochu, and kome-jochu according to their ingredients.

ロック
on the rocks

水割り
shochu mixed with water

お湯割り
shochu mixed with hot water

チューハイ
shochu and soda

Dining manners

* Ramen

ラーメン

ラーメンのスープの味には、しょうゆ、塩、みそ、とんこつがあります。
Ramen soup is seasoned with soy sauce, salt, miso, and pork.

麺は太めと細めなどがあります。ゆで加減などが指定できる店もあります。
There are thin and thick noodles. There are ramen shops where customers can request how hard they would like their noodles to be.

● ラーメンのマナー Manners for eating ramen

音をたててすすってもかまいません。
You can make noises when you eat ramen.

音をたてて食べると温度が下がり、やけどしません。
When you eat ramen, you should slurp noodles so that you don't burn your mouth.

● トッピング Toppings

別料金でトッピングを追加することもできます。
You can pay to add toppings to your ramen.

chashu チャーシュー Chinese-style barbecued pork	nitamago 煮卵 boiled egg	moyashi もやし bean sprout

30

全国のラーメン Ramen in Japan

日本各地に地域の名を冠した特徴的なラーメンがあって、人気です。

There are signature varieties of ramen named after the region in Japan where they originate from, and they are popular.

旭川ラーメン
（北海道）
Asahikawa-ramen
(Hokkaido)

札幌ラーメン
（北海道）
Sapporo-ramen
(Hokkaido)

喜多方ラーメン
（福島県）
Kitakata-ramen
(Fukushima)

東京ラーメン
（東京都）
Tokyo-ramen
(Tokyo)

博多ラーメン
（福岡県）
Hakata-ramen
(Fukuoka)

熊本ラーメン
（熊本県）
Kumamoto-ramen
(Kumamoto)

食券 Meal ticket

店頭の食券販売機で食券を買って、注文する店が多いです。

Many shops have vending machines that prints meal coupons. Customers buy these meal tickets from a machine.

Dining manners

✱ Home-cooked Meals

家庭料理

● ご飯 Rice

家庭料理の主食はご飯です。
In home cooking, rice is our staple food.

白米、玄米、五穀米などがあります。
We have white rice, brown rice, and five grain rice
（rice, wheat, foxtail millet, Japanese millet, and millet）.

● みそ汁 Miso soup

だしにみそを加えた汁物です。
Miso soup is soup stock made with miso.

具材は、野菜、豆腐、貝や海藻などがあります。
We add ingredients such as vegetables, tofu, shellfish, and seaweed.

● 漬け物 Pickles

野菜を、塩、酢、しょうゆ、みそなどで漬けたものです。
Vegetables are pickled in salt, vinegar, soy sauce, and soybean paste called "miso".

風味がよく、保存性が高いものです。
It has good flavor and can be stored for a long time.

主な家庭料理 Home-cooked meal

nikujaga
肉じゃが
simmered meat and potatoes

okonomiyaki
お好み焼き
Okonomiyaki is a kind of Japanese-style pancake or pizza.

tori-no-karaage
鳥のから揚げ
fried chicken

buta-no-syogayaki
豚のしょうが焼き
pork stir fry with ginger

yakizakana
焼き魚
grilled fish

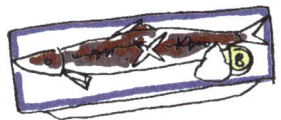

saba-no-misoni
さばの味噌煮
miso-simmered mackerel

kimpira
きんぴら
chopped burdock root and carrot cooked in sugar and soy sauce

potetosarada
ポテトサラダ
potato salad

tamagoyaki
たまご焼き
a sweetened and soy-flavored omelette

Dining manners

✳ Ekiben, Box lunch, and Onigiri
駅弁・弁当・おにぎり

駅弁は、駅や列車の中で売っている弁当で、旅の途中で買って食べます。
Ekiben is sold at stations and on some trains.
People buy them while they travel.

● 有名な駅弁
Famous box lunches sold at railroad stations

makunouchi-bento
幕の内弁当
（全国）

a variety box lunch
(the whole of Japan)

ikameshi
いかめし
（北海道）

squid stuffed
with rice (Hokkaido)

gyutan-bento
牛たん弁当
（宮城県）

box lunch with beef
tongue and rice
(Miyagi)

masuzushi
ます寿司
（富山県）

trout sushi (Toyama)

fukagawameshi-bento
深川めし弁当
（東京都）

rice cooked with
clams (Tokyo)

shiumai-bento
シウマイ弁当
（神奈川県）

box lunch with shumai
(Kanagawa)

● 弁当・おにぎり Box lunch and Onigiri

日本では、学校、会社、行楽での昼食として、弁当を持っていきます。
Japanese people bring it for lunch to school, the office, or when going out on a pichic.

手作りすることも多いですが、スーパーやコンビニなどでも売っています。
Although mothers usually make it, sometimes people buy it at a supermarket or a convenience store.

おにぎりは、ご飯に塩をつけ、中に具を入れて、三角形などに握ったものです。
Onigiri is a food prepared by putting salt on cooked rice, adding fillings, and then forming it into a triangle or other shape.

代表的な具には、梅干、たらこ、おかか、鮭などがあります。
The primarily used ingredients are umeboshi, cod roe, bonito shavings flavored with soy sauce, and salmon.

おにぎりの握り方 How to make onigiri

1 水でぬらした手に塩を少しつけ、ご飯をのせる。
Put a little salt on wet palms. Then put the rice in your hand.

2 ご飯の中央に具をのせる。
Put the filling on the center of rice.

3 両手でご飯を握る。
Press firmly with both hands.

4 ご飯にのりを巻く。
Wrap the onigiri with nori (seaweed).

Dining manners

✱ Japanese Confectionery
和菓子

和菓子とは、日本の伝統的な作り方で作られたお菓子です。
Japanese traditional confectionery is made using Japanese traditional production techniques.

● 和菓子のマナー
Manners of eating japanese confectionery

生菓子は、菓子切りで小さく切りながらいただきます。
You should eat Japanese unbaked cake after cutting it into small pieces with a toothpick used for cutting sweets in tea ceremony.

まんじゅうなどは、手で持っていただきます。
You can take the sweet bun with your hand.

kashikiri
菓子切り
tooth pick used for cutting sweets

● あんこ Sweet bean paste

和菓子の多くに、あんこが使われています。
A lot of Japanese traditional confectioneries are stuffed with bean jam.

あんこの材料は、小豆と砂糖と塩と水です。
The basic ingredients are azuki beans, sugar, salt, and water. We use it for many kinds of Japanese confectionery, such as sweet buns.

tsubu-an
つぶあん
whole bean sweet bean paste

つぶあんと、こしあんがあります。
There are "koshi-an"(smooth paste) and "tsubu-an"(paste containing pieces of azuki beans skin).

koshi-an
こしあん
smooth sweet bean paste

● 主な和菓子 Kinds of Japanese confectionery

namagashi
生菓子
unbaked cake

manju
まんじゅう
a bun with a bean -jam filing

sakuramochi
桜もち
a rice cake filled with sweet bean paste and wrapped in a pickled cherry leaf

daifuku
大福
a soft rice cake filled with sweet bean jam

yokan
ようかん
sweet jelly of azuki beans

monaka
もなか
bean-jam-filled wafers

dorayaki
どら焼き
a bean-jam pancake

dango
だんご
rice-flour dumplings put on bamboo skewers

sembei
せんべい
rice cracker

Dining manners
* Japanese Tea
日本茶

kyusu
急須
small teapot

chaba
茶葉
tea leaf

chawan
茶碗
teacup

栽培の方法や、摘む時季、製造法によって、さまざまな種類の日本茶になります。
We can make different kinds of Japanese tea according to the cultivation processes, harvest time, and manufacturing process.

大きく分けて、煎茶、ほうじ茶、抹茶があります。
Japanese tea is roughly divided into three kinds.
They are ordinary green tea, roasted tea, and powdered tea.

ふつう日本茶といえば、煎茶のことです。
Usually, "Japanese tea" refers to ordinary green tea.

日本茶のおいしいいれ方
How to make delicious Japanese tea

1 急須に茶葉（2人分でティースプーン2杯）を入れます。
Put two spoons of tea leaves in a small teapot.

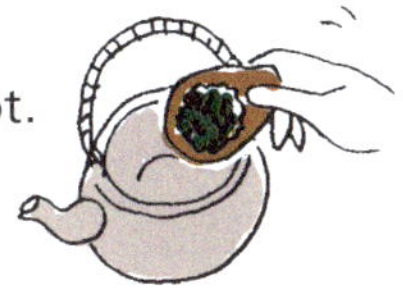

2 茶碗に熱湯を入れ、温度を冷まします。
Pour hot water in a teacup to cool it.

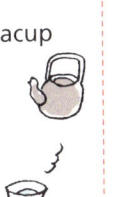

3 茶碗の湯を急須に入れ、30秒おきます。
Pour warm water in a small teapot and leave it for thirty seconds.

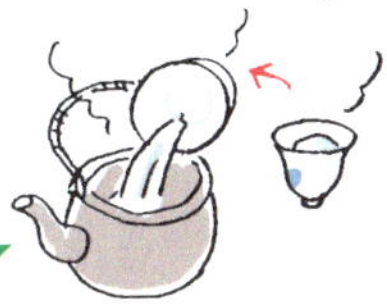

4 茶碗に回し注ぎをし、お茶の濃さを一定にします。
Serve tea evenly little by little into each cup. This makes the strength of the tea the same in each cup.

日本茶のいただき方 How to drink Japanese tea

1 ふたがある場合は、茶碗に左手を添え、右手でふたを取って、つまみを下にして右側に置きます。
Put your left hand on the left side of the teacup and pick up the lid with your right hand. Then put the knob of the lid down on the right side of the teacup.

2 茶托から右手で茶碗を持ち上げ、左手を添えます。
Pick up the teacup from the teacup saucer with your right hand and support it with the left.

3 ひと口飲んだら、茶托に戻します。
After taking a sip, put the teacup on the teacup saucer.

Manners for staying and visiting

✳ Japanese-style Hotels (Ryokan)

日本旅館

● 日本旅館に泊まる
Staying at a Japanese-style hotel

仲居さんが、部屋に案内してくれます。
Waitresses in a ryokan make tea and explain the details of the ryokan.

部屋には、お茶とお茶菓子が用意してあります。
There are a teapot and sweets in the room.

夕食と朝食は、部屋に運んでくれる場合、食堂で食べる場合があります。
You can eat dinner and breakfast in your room or in the restaurant.

布団を敷いたり上げたりするのは、従業員がしてくれます。
The futons are spread and folded up by the ryokan staff.

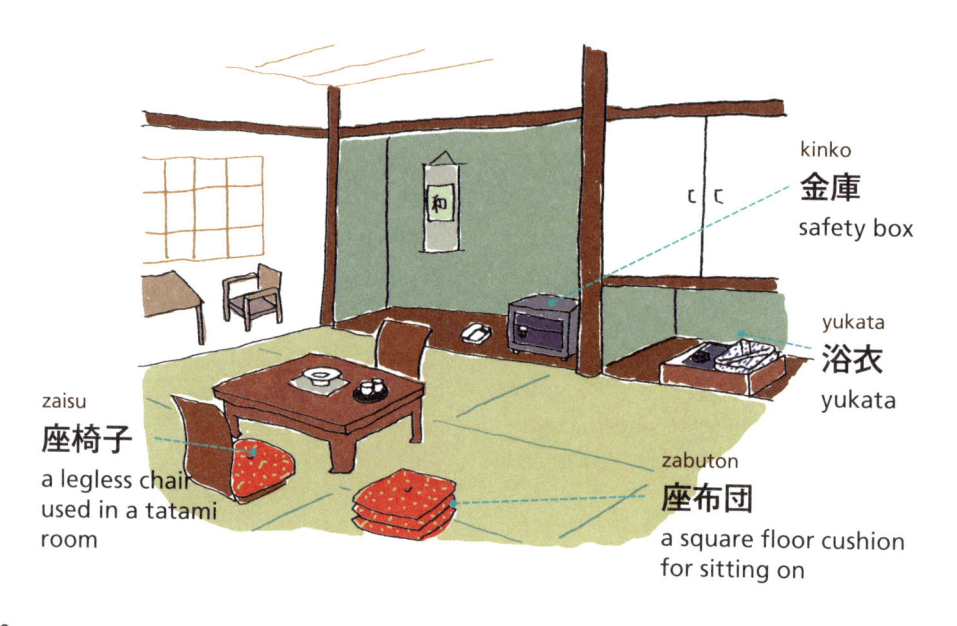

kinko
金庫
safety box

yukata
浴衣
yukata

zaisu
座椅子
a legless chair used in a tatami room

zabuton
座布団
a square floor cushion for sitting on

旅館の浴衣の着方
How to wear a yukata in a Japanese-style hotel

旅館では、用意してある浴衣に着替えてくつろぎます。
People feel relaxed by wearing a yukata provided by a Japanese-style hotel.

1 えりは右を下に、左を上に重ねます。
Wear with the left side folded over the right side.

2 腰に帯を締めます。
Tie with a belt around your waist.

NG えりを左右逆に重ねると、亡くなった人の着方になるので注意しましょう。
A dead person is dressed in a kimono with the right side folded over the left side.

日本旅館の楽しみ
Enjoyment of staying at a Japanese-style hotel

ゲームコーナー、カラオケ、卓球台などがある旅館もあります。
Some of them have a video game arcade, karaoke, and ping-pong.

土産物コーナーでは、地方の特産品を売っています。
They sell local specialties at the souvenir shop.

Manners for staying and visiting

✱ Hot Springs

温泉

全国に3000以上の温泉地があります。
There are more than 3,000 hot springs in Japan.

温泉には、皮膚病、冷え性、肩こり、疲労回復など、さまざまな効能があります。
They are good for skin ailments, chills, stiff shoulder, fatigue, and so on.

● 主な温泉 Famous hot springs

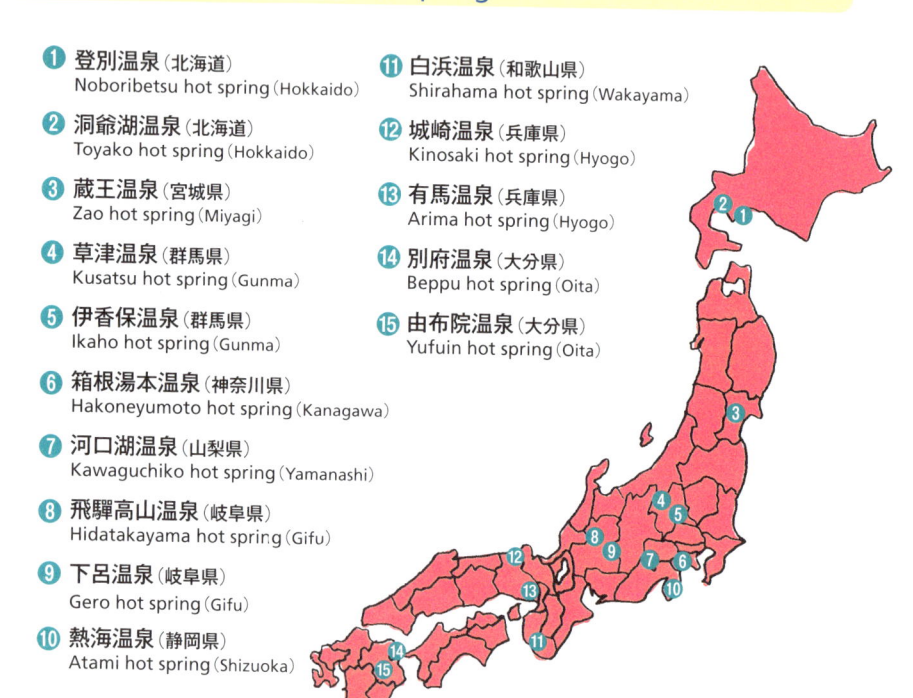

❶ 登別温泉(北海道)
Noboribetsu hot spring (Hokkaido)

❷ 洞爺湖温泉(北海道)
Toyako hot spring (Hokkaido)

❸ 蔵王温泉(宮城県)
Zao hot spring (Miyagi)

❹ 草津温泉(群馬県)
Kusatsu hot spring (Gunma)

❺ 伊香保温泉(群馬県)
Ikaho hot spring (Gunma)

❻ 箱根湯本温泉(神奈川県)
Hakoneyumoto hot spring (Kanagawa)

❼ 河口湖温泉(山梨県)
Kawaguchiko hot spring (Yamanashi)

❽ 飛騨高山温泉(岐阜県)
Hidatakayama hot spring (Gifu)

❾ 下呂温泉(岐阜県)
Gero hot spring (Gifu)

❿ 熱海温泉(静岡県)
Atami hot spring (Shizuoka)

⓫ 白浜温泉(和歌山県)
Shirahama hot spring (Wakayama)

⓬ 城崎温泉(兵庫県)
Kinosaki hot spring (Hyogo)

⓭ 有馬温泉(兵庫県)
Arima hot spring (Hyogo)

⓮ 別府温泉(大分県)
Beppu hot spring (Oita)

⓯ 由布院温泉(大分県)
Yufuin hot spring (Oita)

● 温泉のマナー Manners of hot springs

湯船に入る前に、かけ湯を浴びて、身体をサッと洗い流します。
Before you soak in the tub, you wash roughly by pouring hot water over your body.

長い髪はまとめて、お湯につけないようにします。
You should tie up long hair so that it does not soak it in the bathtub.

湯船には、タオル、シャンプー、石けんを入れてはいけません。
You can't put towels, shampoo bottles, or soap in the tub.

湯船の中で、身体を洗ってはいけません。
You can't wash your body in the tub.

洗濯をしてはいけません。
You can't wash your clothing in the tub.

大声で騒いではいけません。
You can't make a lot of noise.

隣の人にお湯をはねかけないように注意します。
You have to pay attention not to splash hot water on the person next to you.

使ったいすや手桶は、さっと洗って元の場所に戻します。
Roughly wash the chair and the pail you used.

2 宿泊・訪問のマナー

Manners for staying and visiting

✱ Public Baths

銭湯

onnayu
女湯
women's bath

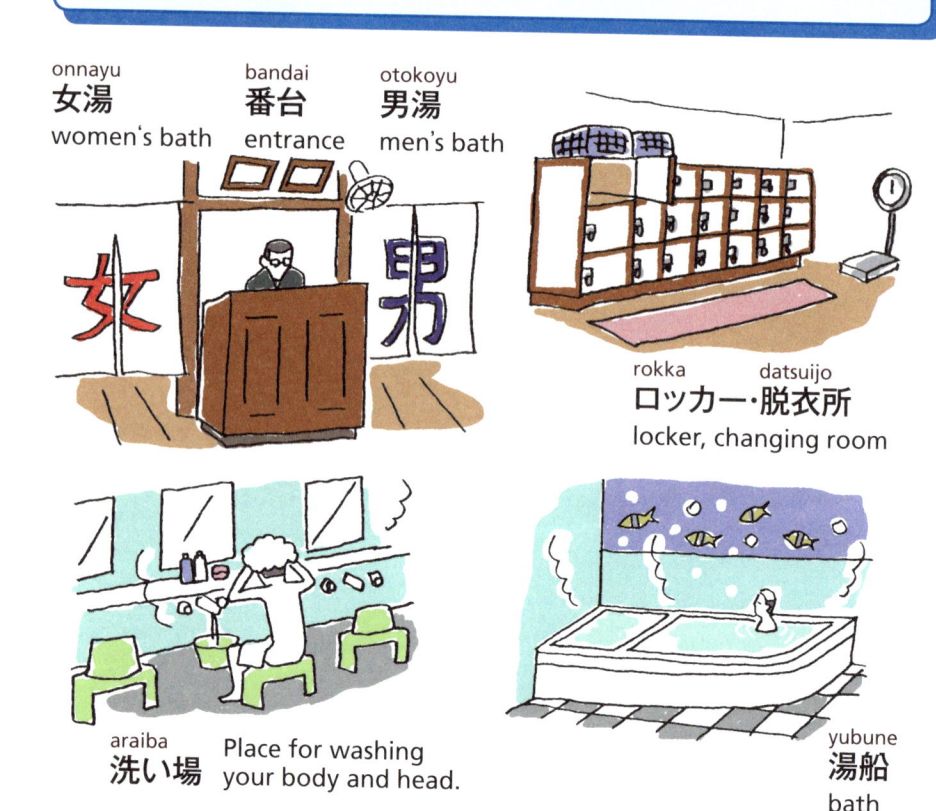

bandai
番台
entrance

otokoyu
男湯
men's bath

rokka   datsuijo
ロッカー・脱衣所
locker, changing room

araiba
洗い場　Place for washing your body and head.

yubune
湯船
bath

銭湯は、町中にある大衆浴場です。

A sento is a public bath that be found around town.

男湯と女湯に分かれています。

The women's bath and the men's bath here are separated.

多くの銭湯で、壁に富士山と海の絵が描かれています。

A beautiful picture of Mt. Fuji and the sea is on the wall of the bathing area.

44

● 銭湯の入り方 How to take a bath

1 靴を脱いで下駄箱に入れます。
鍵をなくさないように注意。
Take off your shoes and put them in the shoe locker. Make sure you don't lose your key.

getabako
下駄箱
shou locker

▽

2 受付（番台）で先に料金を払います。
Pay the entrance fee at the reception desk (bandai).

▽

3 脱衣所で衣服をすべて脱ぎます。
Take off your all clothing in the dressing room.

▽

4 脱いだ衣服はロッカーに入れます。
Put your clothing in the locker.

▽

5 湯船に入る前に、洗い場で身体を洗います。
You have to wash your body before getting into the bath.

▽

6 サウナに入るときは、身体をふいてからにします。
Before entering the sauna, you should dry off your body.

▽

7 上がるときは、身体をよくふいて、脱衣所をぬらさないようにします。
Dry your body before going back to the locker&changing room.

Manners for staying and visiting

✳ Shukubos

宿坊

宿坊は仏教の寺院の地区内や周辺にあり、僧侶や参拝者のための宿泊施設です。
A shukubo is a form of lodging for priests who are conducting ascetic practices and for visitors, and they are found mainly in Buddhist temples.

寺院の1日の勤めに合わせて、規則正しいスケジュールが必要なことも多くあります。
People often spend a day with a regular schedule related to the religious service of a Buddhist temple.

比較的安い料金で、一般の人も利用できます。
People can stay there for a relatively inexpensive fee.

● 精進料理 Shojin-ryori

精進料理が味わえる宿坊もあります。
Some shukubos serve luxirious shojin-ryori.

精進料理とは、仏教の戒律にもとづいた、魚や肉を使わない料理です。
Shojin-Ryori are dishes made without fish or meat, based on Buddhist commandments.

坐禅・瞑想
Zazen and meditation

宿坊の禅宗のお寺では坐禅、真言宗のお寺では瞑想が体験できます。

You can experience zazen at the temple, and meditation at a Shingon sect temple.

写経・滝修行
Shakyo and takigyo

お経を書き写す写経や、滝に身を打たれる滝修行ができる宿坊もあります。

There are some shukubos where you can do shakyo (making a handwritten copy of a sutra) or takigyo (meditation by sitting under a water fall).

朝のお勤め
Morning religious service

朝早く、住職が仏様にお経を唱えます。

The chief priest chants a Buddhist sutra early in the morning.

仏像を見たり、庭を眺めることもできます。

You can see Buddha statues and the garden.

Manners for staying and visiting

✳ Japanese Houses

日本の家

❶ 床の間　tokonoma
❷ 押入れ　oshiire
❸ 鴨居　kamoi
❹ 障子　syoji
❺ 縁側　engawa
❻ 敷居　shikii
❼ 畳　tatami
❽ ふすま　fusuma

48

● 神棚 Kamidana (Household Shinto altar)

神道の神をまつるための棚です。

Shinto gods are enshrined on the kamidana.

左右にサカキ、灯明(とうみょう)を配し、
前方に注連縄(しめなわ)をかけます。

Sakaki (sacred evergreens), and tomyo (votive lights) are arranged in front of the kamidana, and shimenawa (sacred rice straw ropes) are hung in front of them.

注連縄
shimenawa

サカキ
sakaki

● 仏壇 Butsudan (Buddhist altar)

仏壇は、家の中にある仏をまつる厨子(ずし)であり、家族の死者をまつる祭壇でもあります。

A butsudan is a permanent miniature temple in an ordinary house to enshrine Buddha, and it also serves as an alter to enshrine the ancestors of the family.

お花を飾(かざ)ったり、お供物を捧げたり、お線香を焚(た)きます。

We put flowers, and offerings here, and also burn incense sticks here.

hana
花
flowers

senko
線香
incense sticks

● 床の間 Tokonoma (Alcove in a traditional Japanese room where art or flowers are displayed)

座敷の上座にあたる部分で、床が一段高くなっています。

Tokonoma is the spot of a tatami room which is called "kamiza". It is an elevated alcove.

壁には掛け軸、床には花や置物が置かれます。

We put kakejiku (a hanging scroll) on the wall and display flowers on the floor.

花
flowers

掛け軸
kakejiku

2 宿泊・訪問のマナー

49

Manners for staying and visiting

✲ Visiting Someone's House
訪問

● **玄関での挨拶** Greeting at the entrance

玄関に入る前に、コートを脱ぎます。
You should take off your coat before entering a house.

玄関での挨拶は簡単にします。
Your greeting at the entrance should be simple.

靴の脱ぎ方、そろえ方 How to take off your shoes

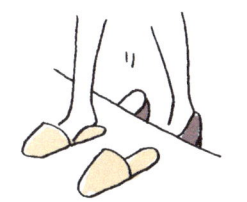

1 正面を向いたまま、靴を脱ぎます。
You should take off your shoes facing the toward the house.

2 斜めにかがみ、靴の向きを変えてそろえます。
Crouch sideways and turn your shoes around.

3 そろえた靴を、すみへ置きます。
Put them in a corner.

NG

畳のヘリを、踏まないようにしましょう。
Try not to step on the edge of tatami.

敷居を踏んではいけません。
You must not step on the threshold.

帰るときの挨拶 Greetings for saying "Good-bye".

「今日はありがとうございました」
Thank you for today.

「失礼いたします」
See you soon.

「またいらしてくださいね」
I'm looking forward to you visiting again.

Manners for staying and visiting

✴ Hospitality Gifts

手土産

家に招かれたら、手土産を持っていく習慣があります。

When you are invited to someone's house, you should bring a hospitality gift with you. This is a Japanese custom.

● 選び方のポイント How to choose it

菓子などの軽い食べ物がよいでしょう。

Light food like sweets are a good idea.

家族全員で楽しんでいただけるものにします。

The gift should be the one which the host can enjoy it with his (or her) family.

訪問先の駅前などで買わないようにします。

You shouldn't buy the gift at the shop near your host's house.

手渡すタイミングと渡し方
When and how to hand it

座敷や居間に通されたら、正式な挨拶をしたあと、手土産を渡します。
When you go in the living room or zashiki room, you should make the formal greetings. Then you should present the gift.

「どうぞおかけください」
Please take your seat.

「本日は、お招きありがとうございます」
Thank you for inviting me today.

「心ばかりですが」
This is a small gift.

紙袋に入っている場合の渡し方
How to hand a gift in the paper bag

紙袋から出し、相手に正面を向けて手渡します。
Take out the gift from the paper bag and hand it to the host with its front facing the host.

紙袋はたたんで、持ち帰ります。
Keep the paper bag and bring it back to your home.

Manners for worshipping and sightseeing

✱ Shrines

神社

神社とは、日本固有の宗教である、神道の神様がまつられている場所です。
A shrine is a place where Shinto gods are worshipped. Shinto is the indigenous religion of Japan.

日本全国で8万以上の神社があります。
There are more than eighty thousand shrines in Japan.

お正月には、多くの人たちが初詣(はつもうで)をします。
On New Year's Day, many people visit a shrine to pay their first visit of the year.

● 神主と巫女 Shinto priest and a lady

神社には、神職の「神主(かんぬし)」と、神に仕える「巫女(みこ)」がいます。
At the Shinto shrine, there is a man who serves a god called a Shinto priest and a lady who serves a god called a miko.

kannushi
神主
shinto priest

miko
巫女
shinto lady

54

● 有名な神社 Famous Shinto shrines

❶ 日光東照宮（栃木県）
　Nikkotoshogu（Tochigi）
❷ 明治神宮（東京都）
　Meijijingu（Tokyo）
❸ 鶴岡八幡宮（神奈川県）
　Tsurugaokahachimangu
　（Kanagawa）
❺ 下鴨神社（京都府）
　Shimogamojinjya（Kyoto）
❾ 太宰府天満宮（福岡県）
　Dazaifutemmangu（Fukuoka）

❻ 伏見稲荷大社（京都府）
　Fushimiinaritaisha（Kyoto）

❽ 出雲大社（島根県）
　Izumotaisha（Shimane）

❹ 伊勢神宮（三重県）
　Isejingu（Mie）

❼ 厳島神社（広島県）
　Itsukushimajinjya（Hiroshima）

3 参拝・観光のマナー

Manners for worshipping and sightseeing

✻ Worship at a Shinto Shrine
神社の参拝

● 神社参拝のマナー
Manners of worship at a shrine

1 torii
鳥居

神社の入り口には鳥居があります。
鳥居の前で軽く礼をします。

There is a gateway at the entrance to a Shinto shrine. You should give a little bow in front of the Torii.

▽

2 sando
参道

神様が通る中央は避け、
端を通って進みます。

The middle part of the sando is the path for the god. You shouldn't walk there.

▽

3 cyozuya
手水舎

参拝の前に、身を清めます (➡p.63)。
You should wash your hands before worship.

▽

56

4 鈴 (suzu)

軽く礼をして、鈴を鳴らします。鈴には、邪気をはらう力があるといわれています。
Give a little bow and ring the bell. The bell has the power to purge feeling of malice.

▽

5 お賽銭 (osaisen)

お賽銭箱にお金を入れます。
Throw money into the offertory box.

▽

6 二礼二拍手一礼 (nirei-nihakushu-ichirei)

深いおじぎを2回します。
Bow low twice.

胸の高さで拍手を2回し、手を合わせます。
Put both hands together in front of your chest and clap twice.

最後に、深いおじぎを1回します。
Bow low once at the end.

※神社によって異なる場合があります。
These manners differ depending upon the shrine.

Manners for worshipping and sightseeing

✻ Sacred lots and Charms

おみくじ・お守り

神社やお寺では、おみくじやお守りなどを買うことができます。
You can buy a sacred lots or a charm at shrine or temple.

● おみくじ Sacred lots

おみくじは、紙に書かれた、吉凶を占うくじです。
Omikuji is a written fortune that tells you your fortune.

おみくじが凶の場合は、木に結ぶと、凶が吉になるといわれています。
It is said that when a bad one is drawn it should be tied to the branch of tree in order to change it from bad to good.

● おみくじの見方
How to interpret the sacred lots

daikichi
大吉 excellent luck
kichi
吉 average good luck
chukichi
中吉 moderate good luck
shokichi
小吉 lesser good luck

suekichi
末吉 future good luck
kyo
凶 bad luck
daikyo
大凶 greater bad luck

● お守り Charm

持っている人に幸運や良縁をもたらし、
邪気をはらうためのものです。

Omamori are charms that bring good fortune and expel evil.

● お札 Ofuda

家内安全、五穀豊穣などを願って、
家の中などにまつるものです。

People worship ofuda while praying for the safety of their family or the productiveness of grain.

● 絵馬 Ema

受験合格や良縁などを願って、願いごとと名前を
書いて奉納する、絵が描かれた木の板です。

An ema is a wooden board with a picture of a horse, upon which people write their name and a wish. It is dedicated to a temple or a shrine.

● 破魔矢 Hamaya

矢の形をした、正月の縁起物。
悪いものを射してくれるといわれています。

A hamaya is an arrow given as a lucky charm at the New Year. People say a hamaya can kill evil spirits.

Manners for worshipping and sightseeing

✳ Temples

お寺

お寺の宗教は、仏教です。
Temples represent Buddhism.

仏教は、インドから中国を経て、6世紀に日本へ伝わりました。
Buddhism originated in India, and was transmitted to China. Then it was transmitted to Japan in the sixth century.

敷地内に、お墓があるお寺も多いです。
There are many temples that have a graveyard.

● 僧侶と尼 Buddhist monks and nuns

お寺の僧侶と尼は、出家して仏教の修行をしています。
Buddhist monks and nuns are the people who have renounced the world and entered the priesthood to practice Buddhistic austerities.

soryo
僧呂
Buddhist monk

ama
尼
Buddhist nun

● 有名なお寺 Famous temples

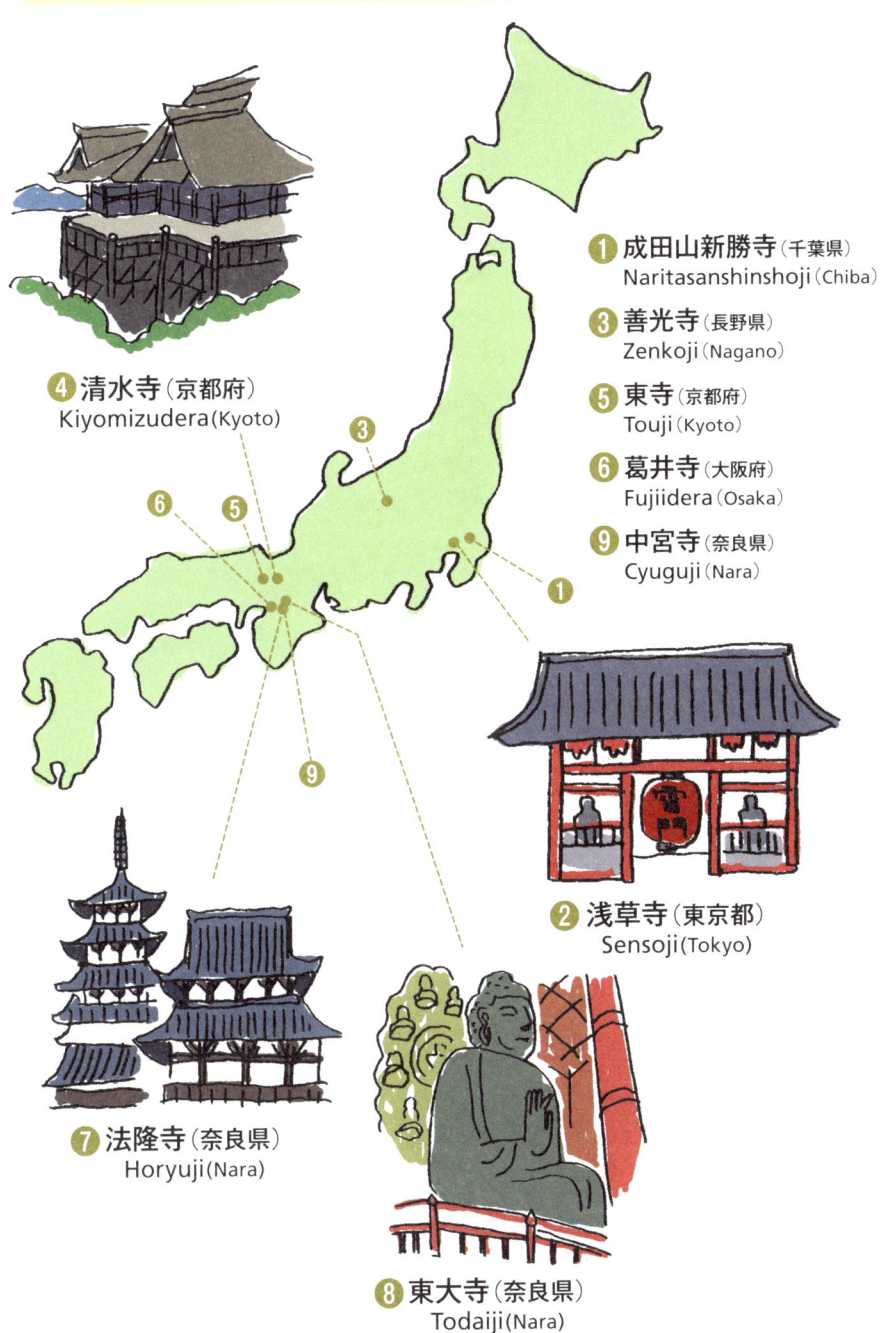

❶ 成田山新勝寺（千葉県）
Naritasanshinshoji (Chiba)

❸ 善光寺（長野県）
Zenkoji (Nagano)

❺ 東寺（京都府）
Touji (Kyoto)

❻ 葛井寺（大阪府）
Fujiidera (Osaka)

❾ 中宮寺（奈良県）
Cyuguji (Nara)

❹ 清水寺（京都府）
Kiyomizudera (Kyoto)

❷ 浅草寺（東京都）
Sensoji (Tokyo)

❼ 法隆寺（奈良県）
Horyuji (Nara)

❽ 東大寺（奈良県）
Todaiji (Nara)

3 参拝・観光のマナー

61

Manners for worshipping and sightseeing

✻ Worship at a Temple
お寺の参拝

● お寺参拝のマナー
Manners for worship at a temple

1 sammon
山門

お寺の入り口は山門です。山門の前で礼をし、敷居は踏まずにまたぎます。

The sanmon is the entrance of a temple. Bow in front of the sanmon and enter the temple without stepping on the shikii.

▽

2 chozuya
手水舎

神社の参拝と同じように、参道の端を通り、手水舎で身を清めます。

As you would do at a shrine, walk along the roadside, then wash your hands at a chozuya.

▽

3 kane
鐘

鐘をつくことができる場合は、参拝の前につきましょう。

If you are permitted to toll the bell, you should do it before you worship.

▽

4 お線香
osenko

お線香が用意されている場合は、火をつけて、献香しましょう。

If there are incense sticks, light one and offer it.

▽

5 本堂
hondo

お賽銭を入れて、一礼します。
手を合わせて祈り、再度礼をします。
拍手はしません。

Throw money into the offertory box and bow once. Put your hands together and pray. Then, bow again. You don't need to clap your hands.

3 参拝・観光のマナー

手水舎の作法 Manners of chozuya

1 右手でひしゃくを持ち、水をすくう。
Grasp a ladle with your right hand and scoop some water.

▽

2 左手を洗う。
Wash your left hand.

▽

3 ひしゃくを持ち替え、右手を洗う。
Switch the ladle from your right hand to your left and wash your right hand.

▽

4 再度持ち替え、左の手のひらに水をためる。
Grasp the ladle with your right hand again, then fill water in your left hand.

▽

5 口をすすぐ。
Rinse your mouth.

▽

6 ひしゃくを縦にし、柄の部分に水をかけて洗う。
Hold the ladle vertically and rinse it by pouring some water over its shaft.

▽

7 ひしゃくを伏せて、元に戻す。
Put the cleaned ladle back into place upside down.

Manners for worshipping and sightseeing

* Buddhist Statues

仏像

仏像とは、仏様の姿を表した塑像(そぞう)・彫像(ちょうぞう)です。

Buddhist statues are sculptures of the Buddha.

もともとは、仏教の開祖である、釈迦(しゃか)の姿を模したものでした。

Originally, they represented Shaka, the founder of the religion.

仏像の種類と有名な仏像
kinds of Buddhist statues and famous Buddhist statues

如来 Nyorai

悟りを開いた、最高ランクの仏です。

Nyorai was enlightened and is in a top class of the Buddha.

釈迦三尊像
(釈迦如来、左·薬王如来、右·薬上菩薩)
法隆寺(奈良県)
Shaka Sanzon-zo
Shakanyorai
left=Yakuonyorai
right=Yakujobosatsu
Horyuji (Nara)

菩薩 Bosatsu

如来をめざして修行に励んでいる仏です。

Bosatsu is a disciplinant who tries to become Nyorai.

十一面千手千眼観世音菩薩
葛井寺（大阪府）
Juichimensenjusengen kanzeombosatsu
Fujiidera (Osaka)

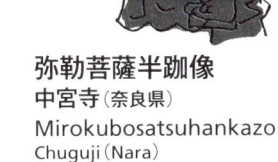

弥勒菩薩半跏像
中宮寺（奈良県）
Mirokubosatsuhankazo
Chuguji (Nara)

明王 Myoo

怒りの形相で、人々を導く仏です。

Myoo lead people with an angry look.

不動明王坐像
東寺（京都府）
Fudomyoozazo
Toji (Kyoto)

天部 Ten-bu

仏教を守る、もともとは古代インドの神々です。

They are originally the gods in ancient India that defended Buddhism.

金剛力士像
東大寺南大門（奈良県）
Kongorikishizo
Todaijinandaimon (Nara)

3 参拝・観光のマナー

Manners for worshipping and sightseeing

✻ Zazen

坐禅

坐禅とは、姿勢を正して座り、沈思黙考し、無の境地に入ることです。

Zazen is a training in Zen Buddhism, in which one meditates deeply while sitting in a correct posture, in order to enter a spiritual state of nothingness.

禅の基本的な修行法のひとつで、いまでもお寺などで体験することができます。

It is a fundamental method of training in Zen Buddhism that you can still experience it in temples nowadays.

● 坐禅の座り方 How to sit

坐禅の座り方には2通りあります。

There are two types of zazen sitting postures.

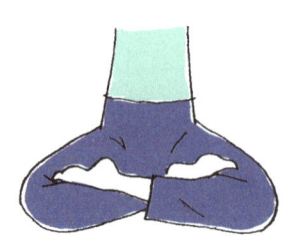

結跏趺坐 kekkafuza

右足は左のももの上に、
左足は右のももの上にのせます。

Sat in Zen meditation with full-lotus.
The right foot is placed on top of the left thigh and the left foot is placed on top of the right thigh.

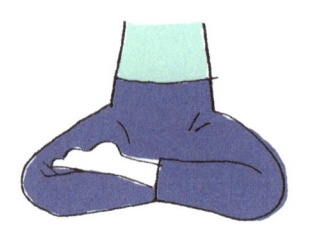

半跏趺坐 hankafuza

片方の足だけを、
もう片方のももの上にのせます。

Sat in Zen meditation with half-lotus.
Only one foot is placed on the opposite thigh.

● 坐禅の基本姿勢 Basic posture of Zazen

右の手のひらの上に左の手のひらを重ね、左右の親指を合わせます。
Place your left hand on your right hand, with your thumbs touching each other.

背筋をぴんと伸ばします。
Keep your back vertical.

目線は斜め下に向け、半分ほど開きます。
Lower your gaze a little. Your eyelids should be half-lowered.

● 警策の受け方 How to receive keisaku

坐禅中、雑念が入ったり、眠くなったりすると、警策で肩を打たれます。
A keisaku is given only those who feel distracted or sleepy during zazen.

1 右肩に警策があてられたら、打たれる前の合図です。
If you feel keisaku on your right shoulder, it is the sign that you will be hit by the keisaku.

▽

2 合掌（がっしょう）してから、首を左に傾け、前傾姿勢になって、警策を受けます。
You join your hands in prayer, tilt your head to the left, and have a head forward posture. Then, you will receive keisaku.

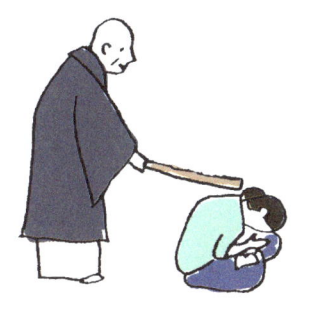

Manners for worshipping and sightseeing

✳ Shakyo

写経

写経とは、仏教のお経（般若心経（はんにゃしんぎょう）など）を書き写すことで、修行のひとつです。
Shakyo is a Buddhist practice of copying Buddhist scriptures (Ex: Hannya-shingyo). This is one of the religious trainings.

それは、大願成就の祈願からはじまりました。
The reason it started was to make his big dream come true.

正式には、筆と墨を使って書き写します。
Formally, people copy sutra with ink and an ink brush.

お寺の中には、道具が用意されていて、写経を体験できるところもあります。
Some temples have shakyo tools for visitors. You can experience it there.

tehon
手本
sample

fude
筆
brush

sumi
墨
ink

68

● 写経の仕方 How to do shakyo

1 正座をして呼吸をととのえ、
心を落ち着かせて行います。

Sit erect with your legs folded under your body and breath in a natural, rhythmical way. Calm your mind.

▽

2 写経の前に、般若心経を唱えます
（わからなければ省略してかまいません）。

Chant the Hannya-shingyo sutra before starting shakyo. (If you don't know it, You don't have to do it.)

▽

3 お経が薄く印刷してありますので、
それを上からなぞっていきます。手本を
下に置いて、模写をする場合もあります。

A Buddhist sutra is printed lightly on a sample copy. You can trace it.
You can put a sample copy under your paper and copy it.

般若心経全文 Entire text of Hannya-shingyo

摩訶般若波羅蜜多心経
観自在菩薩行深般若波羅蜜多時照見五
蘊皆空度一切苦厄舎利子色不異空空不
異色色即是空空即是色受想行識亦復如
是舎利子是諸法空相不生不滅不垢不浄
不増不減是故空中無色無受想行識無眼
耳鼻舌身意無色声香味触法無眼界乃至
無意識界無無明亦無無明尽乃至無老死
亦無老死尽無苦集滅道無智亦無得以無
所得故菩提薩埵依般若波羅蜜多故心無
罣礙無罣礙故無有恐怖遠離一切顛倒夢
想究竟涅槃三世諸仏依般若波羅蜜多故
得阿耨多羅三藐三菩提故知般若波羅蜜
多是大神咒是大明咒是無上咒是無等等
咒能除一切苦真実不虚故説般若波羅蜜
多咒即説咒曰
羯諦　羯諦　波羅羯諦　波羅僧羯諦
菩提娑婆訶　　般若心経

Manners for worshipping and sightseeing

＊ Japanese Gardens

日本庭園

日本庭園は、美しい自然の風景を再現してつくられています。
Japanese gardens are constructed to re-create beautiful natural scenery.

● 日本庭園の種類 Types of Japanese garden

池泉式庭園 chisenshikiteien
池や小川がある庭園。
There are a pond and a stream in the garden.

枯山水 karesansui
水を使わず、山水を表現した庭園。
This garden expresses hills and waters without using water.

露地 roji
草庵式の茶室の庭園。
The garden of the Soan teahouse.

● 日本庭園にあるもの Objects in a Japanese garden

築山
tsukiyama

庭石
niwaishi

石灯籠
ishidoro

ししおどし
shishiodoshi

茶室
chashitsu

東屋
azumaya

3 参拝・観光のマナー

● 有名な日本庭園 Famous Japanese gardens

桂離宮（京都府）
Katsurarikyu (Kyoto)

足立美術館（島根県）
Adachi museum (Shimane)

Manners for worshipping and sightseeing

✻ Castles

城

日本の城とは、大名たちの戦略の拠点であり、防衛の要でもありました。
Japanese castles were places where daimyos plotted strategies, and they were the key places for defense.

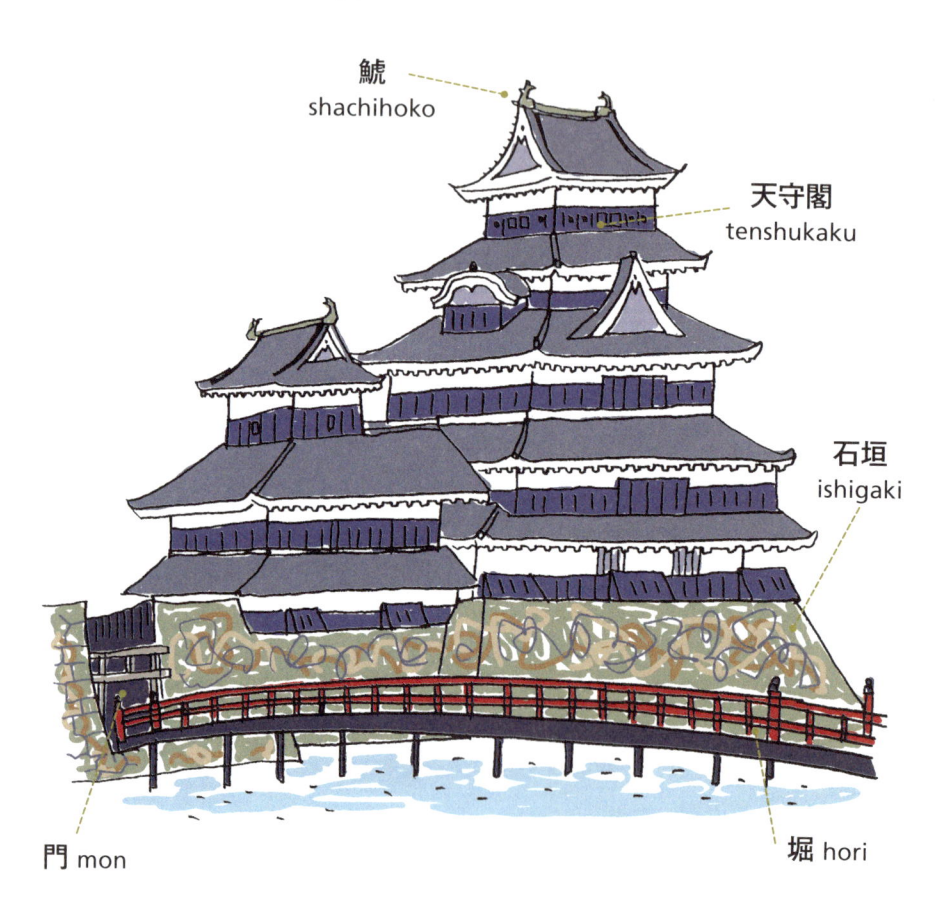

鯱 shachihoko

天守閣 tenshukaku

石垣 ishigaki

門 mon

堀 hori

● 有名な城 Famous castle

松前城（北海道）
Matsumae-jo
(Hokkaido)

弘前城（青森県）
Hirosaki-jo
(Aomori)

名古屋城（愛知県）
Nagoya-jo
(Aichi)

彦根城（滋賀県）
Hikone-jo
(Shiga)

大阪城（大阪府）
Osaka-jo
(Osaka)

姫路城（兵庫県）
Himeji-jo
(Hyogo)

3 参拝・観光のマナー

73

Manners for worshipping and sightseeing

☀ Festivals

祭り

日本の祭りには、繁栄や豊穣(ほうじょう)の祈りがこめられています。
Japanese festivals have prayers for prosperity and fertility.

春と秋は豊作祈願と感謝祭、夏は疫病退散や台風除(よ)けを祈願します。
People hold a fertility and thanksgiving festival in spring and autumn. They pray to ward off evil and to prevent typhoons in summer.

● **祭りの服装** Festival costume

- はちまき hachimaki
- はっぴ happi
- 股引 momohiki
- 足袋 tabi
- 雪駄 setta

● **縁日とは?** What is ennichi (festival day)?

お寺や神社に行くと、
ご利益がある日といわれています。
A festival day is a day on which people go to a shrine and receive a blessing.

縁日では、さまざまな遊びや
食べ物の屋台が並びます。
There are many kind of stands which sell games and food on a festival day.

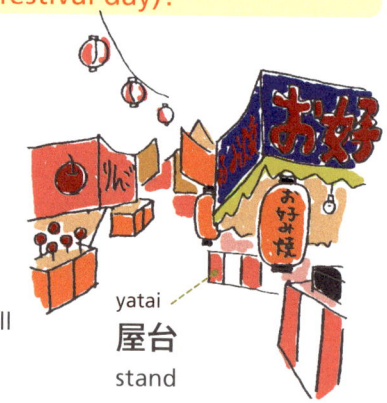

yatai
屋台 stand

山車とみこし
Floats and portable shrines

神社のお祭りでは、皆で山車(だし)を引いたり、みこしを担いだりします。

People pull the floats and carry portable shrines on a festival day at the shrine.

山車やみこしは、「神様の乗り物」といわれています。

It is said that floats and portables shrine are the palanquins for the gods.

mikoshi
みこし
portable shrine

有名な祭り Famous festivals

青森ねぶた祭（青森県・8月）
Aomori-nebuta-matsuri
(Aomori, August)

仙台七夕まつり（宮城県・8月）
Sendai-tanabata-matsuri
(Miyagi, August)

三社祭（東京都・5月）
Sanja-matsuri (Tokyo, May)

博多祇園山笠（福岡県・7月）
Hakatagionyamakasa
(Fukuoka, July)

3 参拝・観光のマナー

75

Manners for worshipping and sightseeing

✳ Cherry Blossom Viewing Parties
花見

日本では、毎年春になると、たくさんの人が桜の花を鑑賞して楽しみます。
Many people enjoy watching cherry blossoms every spring in Japan.

桜が満開になる時期は、地域や気候によって変わります。
The peak bloom date of cherry blossoms differs depending on the area and weather.

桜の花の美しさだけでなく、花が短命ではかないところにも、日本人は魅力を感じています。
Japanese people love cherry blossoms not only their beauty but also for their short lives.

● 桜の種類 Kinds of cherry blossoms

桜にはたくさんの種類があります。
There are many kinds of cherry blossoms.

日本でもっともよく見られるのは、ソメイヨシノです。
The most popular cherry blossom in Japan is someiyoshino.

ソメイヨシノ
someiyoshino

山桜
yamazakura

しだれ桜
shidarezakura

宴会 Party

満開の桜の木の下で、食べたり飲んだり、歌ったりして、楽しみます。

People enjoy singing, eating, and drinking under the cherry blossom trees.

● **花見のマナー**
Manners for cherry blossom viewing

1 シートなどでの場所取りは、人数分だけにします。

If you want to reserve a spot with a plastic sheet, use one that accommodates the number of people in your party.

2 飲みすぎたり、騒ぎすぎたりしないこと。

Don't drink too much or carouse

3 桜の木に登ったり、枝を折ったりしないこと。

Don't climb a cherry blossom tree or cut it down.

4 ゴミは持ち帰ります。

Bring your garbage home with you.

Experience Japanese customs

* Kabuki

歌舞伎

歌舞伎は、江戸時代初期に出雲阿国という女性がはじめて演じたといわれる、400年以上の歴史がある演劇です。

Kabuki is said to have originated from "IZUMO no Okuni," who delivered a performance in the early Edo period. This musical theater style has over 400 years of history.

男性だけで演じられます。

It is performed only by male actors.

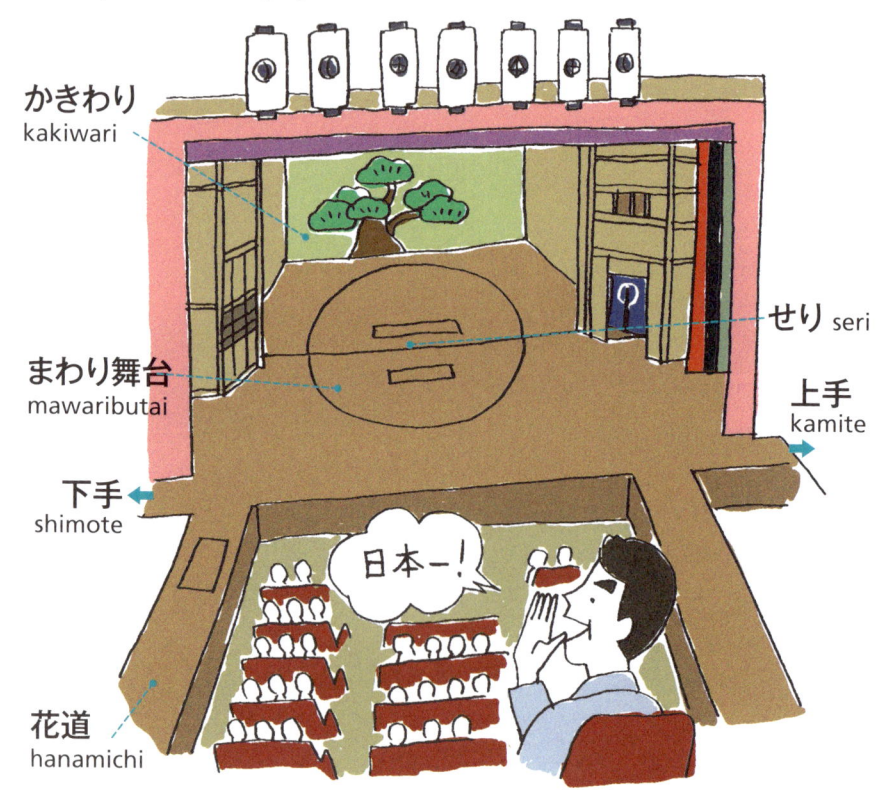

- かきわり / kakiwari
- まわり舞台 / mawaributai
- せり / seri
- 上手 / kamite
- 下手 / shimote
- 花道 / hanamichi

日本一!

78

● 役柄 Cast

女形（女性役）、立役（善人の男性）、荒事師（超人的な力を持つ人）、和事師（色恋に生きる優男）などが登場します。

There are male actors playing female roles, male-roles, heros, as well as soft and clean-cut handsome male role.

● 隈取 Kumadori

顔にほどこす独特の化粧で、役の個性や感情を表現します。

This is the act of using makeup to shade the face and add impact to facial expressions.

● 見栄 Mie

感情が最高潮に達したときに、演技の中で役者が一瞬、行動を停止し、にらむポーズです。

These are stationary poses and gazes that an actor adopts when emotions reach a climax.

● 歌舞伎の観賞 Kabuki viewing

ひとつの演目は数時間に及びます。
It takes a few hours for a drama to finish.

さまざまな演目が、昼、夜、3〜4幕ずつ演じられます。
There are variety of acts. They perform three or four stories at daytime and night.

休憩時間には、飲食をすることができます。
You can have a meal during the intermission.

Experience Japanese customs
✱ Noh

能

能は、14世紀にはじまった、約600年の歴史を持つ音楽劇です。
Noh was established in the 14th century. It's a classical musical drama which has about 600 years of history.

現在も演じられている演劇のうち、世界最古といわれています。
This is the oldest musical drama in the world that is still being performed today.

主役などは、「能面」と呼ばれるお面をつけて演じます。
The main actors put on masks and act.

● **能面** Noh masks

能面には200以上の種類があります。
There are more than 200 kinds of Noh-masks.

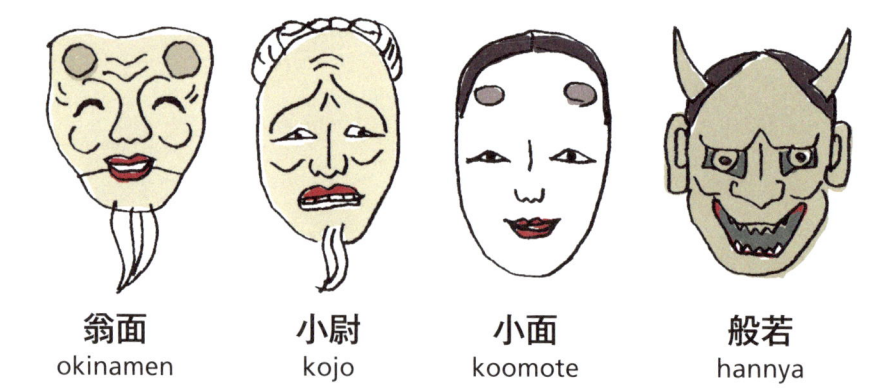

翁面	小尉	小面	般若
okinamen	kojo	koomote	hannya

登場人物 Character of Noh

shite
シテ（主役）
main character

waki
ワキ（脇役）
※狂言では、アドといいます。
supporting character
(They are called "ado").

tsure
ツレ（助演）
support act

囃子方 Hayashikata

楽器を演奏する役です。
This roll plays the instrument.

笛 fue　　**大鼓** otsuzumi　　**小鼓** kotsuzumi　　**太鼓** taiko

狂言とは? What is kyogen?

能と能の間に演じられる「間(あい)狂言」と、独立して演じられる「本(ほん)狂言」があります。

There are two kind of kyogen. One is hon-kyogen which is performed independently. The other is ai-kyogen, which is perfoemed between Noh plays.

風刺や言葉遊びで、日常的な笑いが演じられます。

Kyogen is a comedy based on daily life with satire and word games.

Experience Japanese customs

✳ Kagura

神楽

かぐら
神楽とは、神道の神様に捧げる舞楽です。

Kagura is music and dance dedicated to the Shinto gods.

あまのいわと
天岩戸でアメノウズメが神がかりして舞ったという日本神話が、神楽の起源といわれています。

Kagura had its origin in a Japanese ancient myth of the oracular Amenouzume who had performed a dance in a chapter of Ama no iwato (Cave of heaven).

楽器、歌、舞で構成されます。

It consists of instruments, songs and dance.

● **神楽の面** Kagura masks

面をつけて行われることもあります。

Actors sometimes perform while wearing masks.

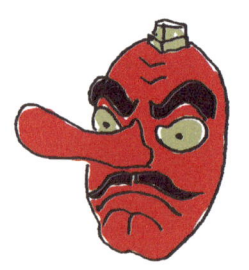

おかめ	ひょっとこ	天狗	きつね
okame	hyottoko	tengu	kitsune

82

Experience Japanese customs

✱ Gagaku

雅楽

雅楽は、1200年以上続いている、宮廷や寺院の音楽と舞です。
Gagaku is court music and dancing which has been performed for more than 1200years.

雅楽独自の楽器が使われます。
They use unique musical instruments.

● 楽器 Instruments

楽箏 gakuso

鉦鼓 shoko

太鼓 taiko

横笛 oteki

和琴 wagoto

楽琵琶 gakubiwa

ひちりき hichiriki

鞨鼓 kakko

笙 sho

4 日本文化にふれる

Experience Japanese customs

＊ Bunraku

文楽

文楽は日本の伝統的な人形劇で、人形浄瑠璃ともいわれます。
Bunraku is a traditional Japanese puppet show called "ningyojoruri".

太夫（語り）、三味線、人形が一体となって演じます。
It is entertainment performed by a tayu (narrator or chanter), shamisen player, and puppeteers.

顔と右手を操る「主遣い」、左手を操る「左遣い」、足を操る「足遣い」の3人で、1体の人形を操ります。
The omozukai manipulates the head and the right hand of the doll.
The hidarizukai manipulates the left hand of the doll.
The ashizukai manipulates the legs of the doll.

● 文楽の舞台 Bunraku stage

omozukai
❶ 主遣い
chief puppeteer

ningyo
❷ 人形
puppet

hidarizukai
❸ 左遣い
left puppeteer

ashizukai
足遣い
legs puppeteer

● 人形のしくみ Build of a doll

人形は肩と腰の部分を布でつないだ胴体に、かしら部分と手足部分を差しこんだ構造になっています。
The trunk of a doll is connected to its shoulder and waist by a cloth. A head, arms, and legs are inserted into it.

かしらにはさまざまな種類があります。
There are many kinds of heads.

源太 genta
二枚目の青年。
handsome young man

傾城 keisei
位の高い遊女。
top ranked prostitute

ガブ gabu
美しい娘が、一瞬にして鬼の形相に変化する頭。
A beautiful girl that changes to a demon in the blink of an eye.

寄席とは？ What is a yose?

落語をはじめ、漫才、講談、手品、曲芸など、さまざまな演芸が見られる場です。
A yose is a small theater where you can enjoy rakugo, manzai, kodan, tejina, and kyokugei.

落語は、一人の演者が座布団の上に座って行う話芸です。
In rakugo a storyteller sits on a mat on stage and tells a well-known funny story.

Experience Japanese customs

✻ Kimonos

着物

着物は、日本の伝統的な民族衣装です。
Kimonos are the national outfit of Japan.

● 着物の正装 Formal dress of kimono

結婚式などのおめでたい席で着られる着物です。
You can wear one during celebratory occasions such as a wedding ceremony.

振袖 furisode
未婚女性の正装の着物です。
This is formal kimono for unmarried young woman.

留袖 tomesode
既婚女性の正装です。
This is formal kimono for married woman.

- 帯揚げ obiage
- 帯 obi
- 帯締め obijime
- おはしょり ohashori
- 草履 zori
- 足袋 tabi

紋つき・羽織・袴 montsuki, haori, hakama
男の人の正装です。背や胸などに、家紋（家を表す印）が入っています。
This is formal Kimono for a man. It has a family crest on the back or the breast.

● 着物のマナー Kimono manners

着物を着たときには、美しい立ち居振る舞いを心がけます。
When you wear a kimono, you should have graceful manners.

歩くとき
When you walk

背筋を伸ばして、
小さめの歩幅で歩きます。

Straighten your back and walk with short steps.

椅子に座るとき
When you sit on the chair

帯がつぶれないように浅く座り、
足先をそろえます。

Sit on the front edge of a chair to maintain the shape of the obi, and keep your feet together

片腕を上げるとき
When you raise one arm

腕がむき出しにならないように、
もう一方の手で袂を押さえます。

Hold the tamoto (the parts that look like bags at the bottom of sleeves) with your hand so that you do not expose your arms.

階段の上り下り
When you go up and down the stairs

すそを踏まないように、右手で着物を
軽くつまんで、つま先に重心をかけて
ゆっくりと進みます。

Pinch the hem of the kimono with your right hand and walk slowly, putting center of gravity over your toes.

4 日本文化にふれる

Experience Japanese customs

* Yukatas

浴衣

浴衣の素材には、たいてい木綿や麻が使われます。夏用の簡易な着物です。
Hemp or cotton is the ordinary material for a yukata.
A yukata is casual kimono for summer.

● 浴衣の着方 How to wear a yukata

女性の浴衣の着方を説明します（男性用は非常に簡単です）。
Explanation of how to wear a yukata (It's very easy for men).

1 浴衣スリップを着ます。
Wear an underwear (yukata-slip) for the yukata.

2 浴衣に袖を通します。
Slip into the yukata.

3 左右のえり先をそろえます。
Hold both collar ends in front of you and check the line.

4 右側を入れ、左側を重ねます。
Bring the left overlap over the right overlap.

5 腰ひもを結びます。
Tie with the koshihimo sash.

6 おはしょりを整えます。
Adjust the ohashori.

7 コーリンベルトを使い、えりの乱れを防ぎます。
Use a korin belt (elastic with plastic clips on both ends) to maintain the shape of the collar.

8 えりの抜きを調整します。
Adjust the distance between the collar and the neck.

9 マジックベルト（伊達締め）を巻きます。
Tie magic belt (datejime) on the top of the koshihimo sash.

着つけ小物セットを買うと、便利です。
It's convenient for you to buy a set of kimono accessories.

10 浴衣帯（作り帯）をつけます。
Wear a yukata obi (tsukuriobi).

着物の柄 Kimono patterns

着物や浴衣には、日本の伝統的な文様が多く用いられています。
Japanese traditional patterns are used for kimonos and yukatas.

麻の葉 asanoha

市松 ichimatsu

七宝 shippo

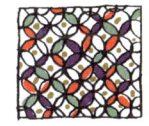

亀甲 kikko

青海波 seigaiha

矢羽根 yabane

Experience Japanese customs

✻ Sado

茶道

茶道は16世紀頃に、千利休が完成したものです。
Tea ceremonies were perfected by Sen-no-Rikyu in the 16th century.

茶碗に抹茶を入れてお湯を注ぎ、茶せんで混ぜて、客に供します。
You pour hot water into a tea bowl, stir the tea with a chasen, then serve the tea to your guest.

茶会では、季節に合わせて用意された、掛け軸や生け花、茶碗などを観賞します。
You can enjoy seasonal wall scrolls flowers, and a tea bowl during a tea ceremony.

❶ 茶碗 chawan
❷ 茶せん chasen
❸ 茶杓 chashaku
❹ 棗 natsume
❺ 建水 kensui
❻ 風炉 furo
❼ 釜 kama
❽ 柄杓 hishaku
❾ 水差し mizusashi

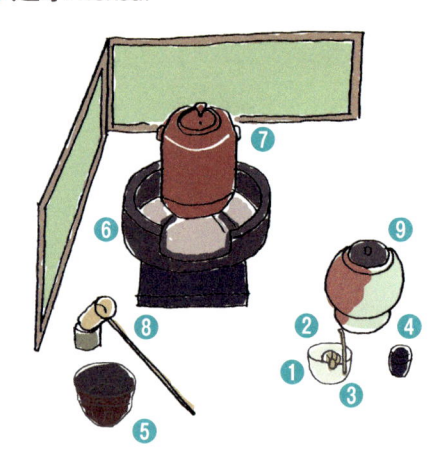

● お茶のいただき方 How to drink tea

1 茶碗を左手にのせ、右手を添えます。
Put the bowl in the palm of your left hand, and hold it with your right hand.

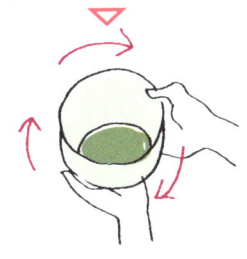

2 茶碗を右に３度回し、お茶を飲みます。
Rotate the bowl clockwise three times, then drink it.

3 最後の１滴は、音を立てて吸います。
Slurp the last drop of tea.

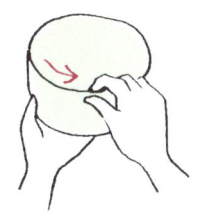

4 飲み口を、人差し指と親指で清めます。指は懐紙でぬぐいます。
Wipe the edge of bowl with your first finger and thumb. Clean your fingers with kaishi.

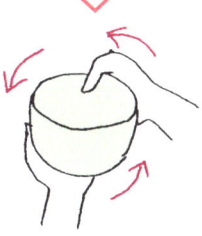

5 茶碗を左に３度回します。
Rotate the bowl counterclockwise three times.

6 感謝の一礼をします。
Bow to express your thanks.

※茶碗を回す回数は、流派によって異なります。
The number of rotations of the bowl is different from ryuha.

Experience Japanese customs

✳ Kado

華道

華道は、16世紀から続く、日本の伝統的な芸術です。
Kado has been a traditional Japanese art since the 16th century.

「いけばな」とも呼ばれます。
People also call it "ikebana".

草木や花の美しさを、花器の上で表現します。
It shows the beauty of vegetation and flowers with a vase.

● 鑑賞のマナー Manners of watching

拝見前とあとに、感謝の一礼をします。
Bow to express your thanks before and after appreciating the flowers.

花から90cmほど離れて鑑賞します。
Stand back about 90cm from the flowers and appreciate them.

全体の構成、花材の組み合わせ、花器、花台などをじっくりと観賞します。
People carefully admire the whole composition, the combination of flowers, the flower vase, and the flower stand.

華道とフラワーアレンジメント
Kado and flower arrangement

華道 Kado

「引き算の美学」といわれ、少ない草木や花を使って、豊かな世界を表現します。

Kado It is called the aesthetics of subtraction. It expresses a rich world with just small amount of vegetation and flowers.

盛り花
moribana

投げ入れ
nageire

バスケット
basket

ブーケ
bouquet

フラワーアレンジメント
Flower arrangement

「足し算の美学」といわれ、たくさんの草花を使って、豪華に活けます。

It is called the aesthetics of addition. Many flowers are arranged gorgeously.

花を活ける技術 Technique of arranging flowers

水切り cut

茎や枝を水中で切り、水を吸いやすくします。

Cut the stems or the twigs under water to increase water absorption.

留める fixing

枝に切りこみを入れ、剣山などに刺しやすくします。

Cut the ends of the branch to insent them into the pinholder easily.

kenzan
剣山 pinholder

4 日本文化にふれる

Experience Japanese customs

✲ Shodo

書道

書道は、毛筆と墨を使って、文字の美を表す芸術です。
Shodo expresses the beauty of characters with a brush and ink stick.

文字を四角く直線で書く「楷書（かいしょ）」、楷書をくずした「行書（ぎょうしょ）」、もっとも自由な書体の「草書（そうしょ）」といった、さまざまな書き方があります。

There are different styles of writing. For example, kaisho (exact style with straight line), gyosho (cursive style) and sosho (barely readable style).

京
楷書
kaisho

● 書道の道具 Calligraphy utensils

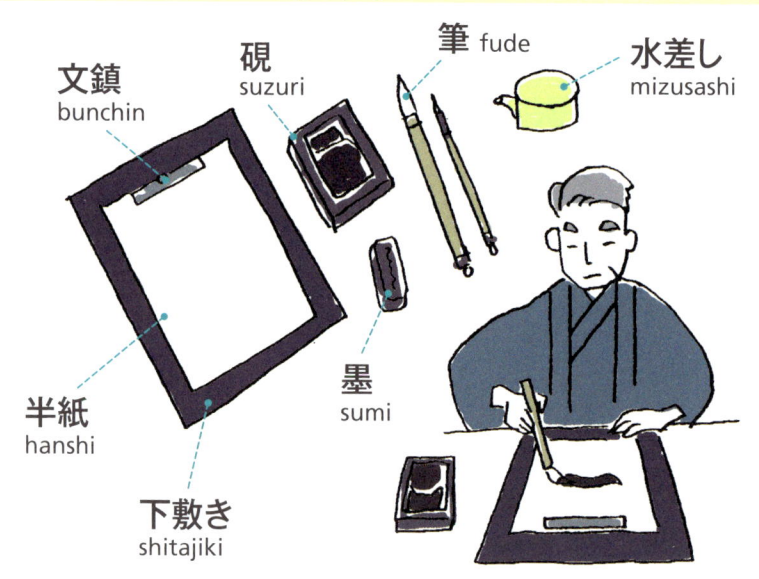

- 文鎮 bunchin
- 硯 suzuri
- 筆 fude
- 水差し mizusashi
- 墨 sumi
- 半紙 hanshi
- 下敷き shitajiki

Experience Japanese customs

✽ Haikus

俳句

俳句は、17音節（5-7-5）で表す日本の詩です。
A haiku is a Japanese poem which consists of 17 syllables （with a 5-7-5 syllables structues）.

俳句には、必ず季語が入ります。
Haikus always contains kigos（words which express a season）.

● 有名な俳句 Famous haikus

春 Spring

古池や
蛙 飛びこむ
水の音

Furuikeya kawazu tobikomu mizu no oto.

The ancient pond, as a frog takes the plunge, sound of the water.

松尾芭蕉 Matsuo Basho

夏 Summer

目には青葉
山ほととぎす
初鰹

Menihaaoba yamahototogisu hatsugatsuo.

Green leaves in eyes, Little cuckoo in mountain, the season's first bonito.

山口素堂 Yamaguchi Sodo

秋 Autumn

柿食へば
鐘が鳴るなり
法隆寺

Kakikueba kaneganarunari Horyuji

I bite a persimmon. I heard the gong Horyu-ji Temple

正岡子規 Masaoka Shiki

冬 Winter

是がまあ
終の栖か
雪五尺

Koregamaa tsuinosumikaka yukigoshaku

Is this my final home？ It has snow 5 shaku （1.515 meters）deep. I can't help but sigh.

小林一茶 Kobayashi Issa

4 日本文化にふれる

Experience Japanese customs

＊ Ukiyoe

浮世絵

浮世絵は、江戸時代に、庶民の間で広まった風俗画です。
A ukiyoe is a type of genre picture which became widely-known in Edo-era.

基本的に、版画となって広まりました。
Basically, ukiyoe pictures became popular via woodblock prints.

ゴッホやモネなど、ヨーロッパの画家にも大きな影響を与えました。
Ukiyoe influenced van Gogh and Claude Monet in Europe.

● 有名な作者と代表作
Famous artists and outstanding works

喜多川歌麿
Kitagawa Utamaro

世界的に有名な美人画の名手です。
He is very famous artist for Bijinga (pictures depicting young women) in the world.

「ビードロを吹く娘」
Bidoro wo fuku musume

「寛政三美人」
Kanseisanbijin

葛飾北斎
Katsushika Hokusai

代表作は「富嶽三十六景」「北斎漫画」など。生涯に3万点もの作品を残しました。

His outstanding works are Fugakusanjurokkei, Hokusaimanga, etc. He drew 30,000 pictures in his life.

「富嶽三十六景・神奈川沖浪裏」
Fugakusanjurokkei・Kanagawaokinamiura

東洲斎写楽
Toshusai Sharaku

10カ月という短い期間に活躍し、こつぜんと姿を消した謎の絵師として知られています。

He is known as a mysterious artist who disappeared suddenly after his lively ten-year period of producing work.

「三世大谷鬼次の奴江戸兵衛」
Sanseiotanionomiji no yakkoedobe

歌川広重
Utagawa Hiroshige

「東海道五十三次」「名所江戸百景」など、風景画のシリーズを手がけました。

He drew landscape paintings, such as Tokaido Gojusantsugi and Meisho Edohyakkei.

「東海道五十三次・日本橋」
Tokaido Gojusantsugi・Nihonbashi

Experience Japanese customs

* Bonsai

盆栽

盆栽は、草木を鉢に植えて仕立てたもので、その姿を鑑賞して楽しみます。
Bonsai is the horticultural art of creating miniature potted tree and plants. People enjoy seeing these.

盆栽でよく使われる代表的な木は、松です。
Pine trees are typically for bonsai.

自然の樹木の美しさや雄大さを、小さな鉢の中で表現しています。
Bonsai expresses the beauty and grandeur of trees in nature in a miniature form.

● よい盆栽の見分け方 How to spot a good bonsai

1 自然の樹木の美しさが表現されている。
It expresses the beauty of trees in nature.

2 盛り上がった根が、あらゆる方向に伸びている。
Its good roots spread in all directions.

3 幹が伸び広がり、大木のような迫力がある。
Its trunk grows out and spread and it is vigorous like a big tree.

4 大きな枝がバランスよく配置されている。
Its big trunk has a good balance.

● 盆栽の形 Shape of bonsai

直幹 chokkan

1本の幹が垂直に伸びた形。
The trunk stools vertically.

模様木 moyogi

幹に変化がある形。
The trunk is twisted into a curved line from left to right.

懸崖 kengai

崖からたれ下がる形。
The trunks and branches grow downwards below the rim of the pot.

● 盆栽作りの技術 Technique of Bonsai making

枝の形を整えるために、針金をかけます。
The trunks are wired to arrange the shape.

ミニ盆栽と苔玉
Mini-Bonsai and Kokedama

10センチ以下の小さなミニ盆栽や、水苔(みずごけ)を丸めて苔を植えた苔玉(こけだま)も、人気があります。
Mini-Bonsai (smaller than 10cm) and Kokedama (moss in rounded peat moss) are also popular.

4 日本文化にふれる

99

Experience Japanese customs

✳ Shikki

漆器

漆器とは、木などに漆(うるし)を塗った、日本の伝統的な工芸品です。
Lacquerware is a wooden craft which is covered with lacquer.
It's a traditional Japanese handicraft.

日本での漆器の歴史はとても古く、9000年前の遺跡から、
漆を使った装飾品が発掘されています。
The history of lacquerware in japan is very old.
An ornament covered with lacquer was found from
remains dating 9000 years ago.

漆を塗ることで、湿気や腐食の防止になります。
Covering the item with lacquer protects it from rotting and humidity.

漆は、ウルシの木の樹液からとれます。
We can extract lacquer from concentrated lacquer-tree sap.

● **漆器を扱うときの注意** How to protect your Shikki

長時間、
水につけない。
Don't put it in
water for a long
time.

直射日光に
あてない。
Don't expose it to
direct light.

電子レンジに
かけない。
Don't warm it up
in the microwave.

食器洗浄機や食器
乾燥機にかけない。
Don't put it in a
dishwasher or
dish dryers.

Experience Japanese customs

✳ Tojiki
陶磁器

日本の陶磁器は古い歴史があり、茶の湯の流行にともなって、独自の特色を持つようになりました。

Japanese tojiki has a long history. It came to have unique features in association with the growth in popularity of Japanese tea ceremonies.

● 主な陶磁器の産地
Main production areas of popular ceramic ware

- ⑨ 備前焼（岡山県） bizenyaki (Okayama)
- ④ 美濃焼（岐阜県） minoyaki (Gihu)
- ③ 九谷焼（石川県） kutaniyaki (Ishikawa)
- ⑩ 萩焼（山口県） hagiyaki (Yamaguchi)
- ⑧ 清水焼（京都府） kiyomizuyaki (Kyoto)
- ① 笠間焼（茨城県） kasamayaki (Ibaraki)
- ⑪ 唐津焼（佐賀県） karatsuyaki (Saga)
- ② 益子焼（栃木県） mashikoyaki (Tochigi)
- ⑤ 瀬戸焼（愛知県） setoyaki (Aichi)
- ⑫ 伊万里・有田焼（佐賀県） imariyaki/aritayaki (Saga)
- ⑥ 常滑焼（愛知県） tokonameyaki (Aichi)
- ⑬ 薩摩焼（鹿児島県） satsumayaki (Kagoshima)
- ⑦ 信楽焼（滋賀県） shigarakiyaki (Shiga)

4 日本文化にふれる

Experience Japanese customs
＊ Sumo Wrestling
相撲

土俵の中で2人の力士が戦う国技です。
Sumo is the national sport of Japan. Two sumo wrestlers fight in a ring.

勝つためには、相手を倒すか、土俵の外に出します。
You win if you make your opponent fall on the floor or push him out of the ring.

日本の国技ですが、最近は外国人の力士が増えています。
Although it's a national sport in Japan, recently there are many foreign wrestlers.

● 力士 Sumo wrestler

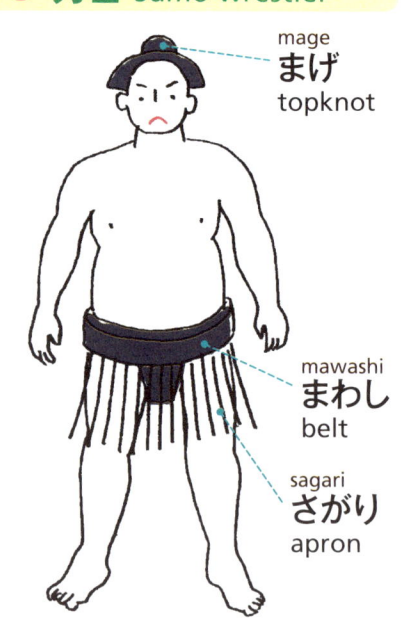

- mage / まげ / topknot
- mawashi / まわし / belt
- sagari / さがり / apron

● 番付 Ranking lists

力士の階級を表した一覧表を「番付」といいます。
Banzuke is the ranking list that shows the ranks of sumo wrestlers.

横綱 yokozuna
大関 ozeki
関脇 sekiwake
小結 komusubi
前頭 maegashira
十両 juryo

相撲の技 Sumo techniques

相撲の技（決まり手）は、全部で82あります。
There are 82 techniques (winning technique) of sumo.

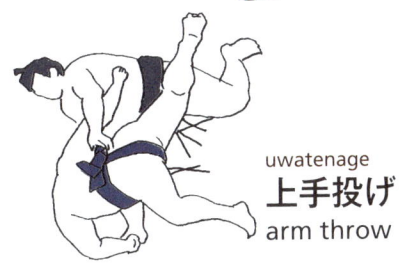

yorikiri
寄り切り
pushing one's opponent out of the ring while holding his belt.

oshidashi
押し出し
pushing out

hatakikomi
はたきこみ
slapping down

uwatenage
上手投げ
arm throw

相撲観戦のマナー
Manners for watching sumo wrestling

服装は自由ですが、帽子は脱ぎます。
There is no dress code, but you should take off your hat.

升席では、相撲茶屋の仕出しで飲食できます。
You can eat and drink items served by Sumo chaya in the box seat.

取り組み中は、座席を移動しないように。
You shouldn't change seats during the bout.

座布団は投げないこと。
You shouldn't throw your zabuton (Japanese cushion).

Experience Japanese customs

✳ Martial Arts

武道

🔴 剣道 Kendo (Japanese art of fencing)

剣道は、防具をつけ、
竹刀を使って1対1で対戦します。

Kendo is a one-on-one martial art in which bamboo swords and protective gear are used.

men
面
mask

shinai
竹刀
bamboo sword

🔴 弓道 Kyudo (Japanese art of archery)

弓道は、的に矢を射て、
あてた本数などを競います。

Kyudo is a martial art in which participants shoot a Japanese arrow at a target and compete on the number of the arrows that hit the target.

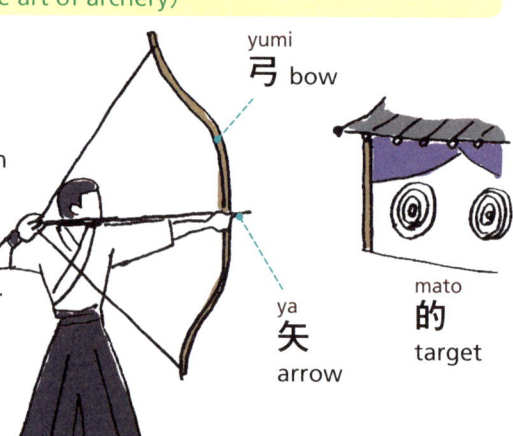

yumi
弓 bow

ya
矢
arrow

mato
的
target

● 柔道 Judo (Japanese art of self-defense)

武具を使わずに、相手を投げる、組みふせる、締める武道です。
Judo is the martial arts in which techniques of throwing and holding down your opponent without the use of weapons are used.

寝技 groundwork techniques

投げ技 throwing techniques

関節技 joints-attack techniques

● 合気道 Aikido (Japanese art of weaponless self-defense)

力を使わず、関節技を利用します。
護身術として知られています。
Aikido doesn't require force, but it relies on the use of joint-locking techniques.
It is known as the art of defense.

● 空手 Karate

「突き・受け・蹴り」が
基本の技です。
The basic techniques are punch, block, and kick.

Experience Japanese customs

✳ Samurais (warriors)

侍

さむらい
侍 は、武士ともいいます。
Samurais are also called "bushi".

侍が政権を持ったのは、鎌倉時代から江戸時代までの670年余りでした。
The samurai government continued from the Kamakura era to Edo era, for a period of 670 years.

戦時は兵士、平時は役人として働きました。
They work as fighters during wartime, and as officers during ordinary times.

● 平時の服装　Clothes in ordinary times

● 戦時の服装　Clothes during wartime

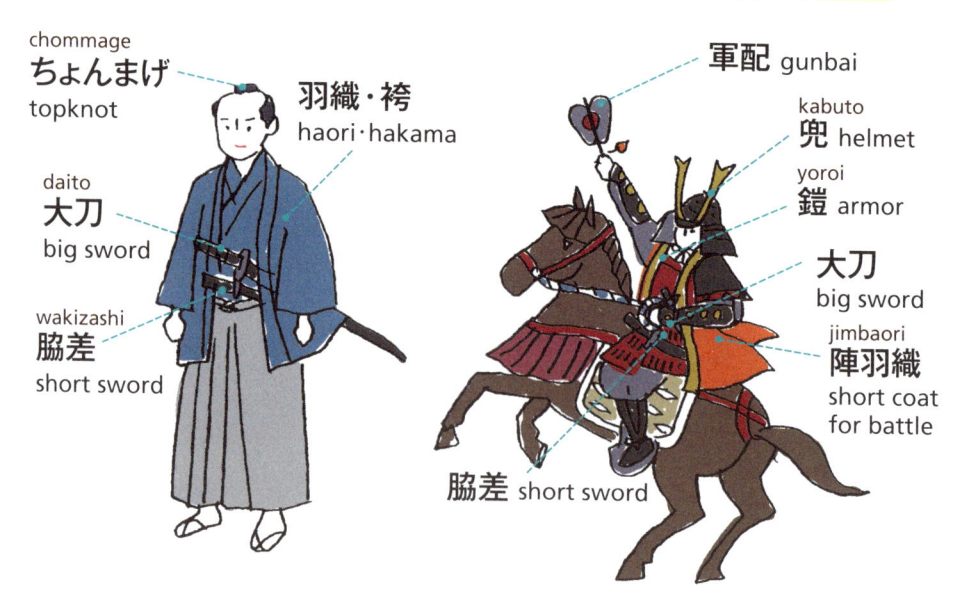

chommage
ちょんまげ
topknot

羽織・袴
haori・hakama

daito
大刀
big sword

wakizashi
脇差
short sword

軍配 gunbai

kabuto
兜 helmet

yoroi
鎧 armor

大刀
big sword

jimbaori
陣羽織
short coat for battle

脇差 short sword

Experience Japanese customs

✱ Ninjas (spies in medieval times in Japan)

忍者

忍者は、忍術を使って、スパイ活動をします。
Ninjas commit espionage by using ninjutsu (ninja martial arts).

伊賀(三重県)と甲賀(滋賀県)で発達した、独自の忍術が使われます。
They use their original ninjyutsu developed in Iga (Mie) and Kouka (Shiga).

● 武器 weapons

shuriken
手裏剣
throwing knife

kunai
くない
Ninjas hold this with one hand and stab an enemy, or they brandish it by putting the cord through the ring.

kusarigama
鎖鎌
a chain and a sickle

makibishi
まきびし
sharp-pointed object scattered on the road.

● 忍術 Ninjutsu (ninja martial arts)

suiton-no-jutsu
水遁の術
Hiding under water

mokuton-no-jutsu
木遁の術
Hiding among the trees

doton-no-jutsu
土遁の術
Hiding and escaping under the ground

katon-no-jutsu
火遁の術
Hiding by using fire

4 日本文化にふれる

Experience Japanese customs

✳ Origami (the Art of Paper Folding)

折り紙

折り紙は、日本の伝統文化です。
Origami is part of Traditional Japanese culture.

● 伝統的な折り紙 Traditional origami

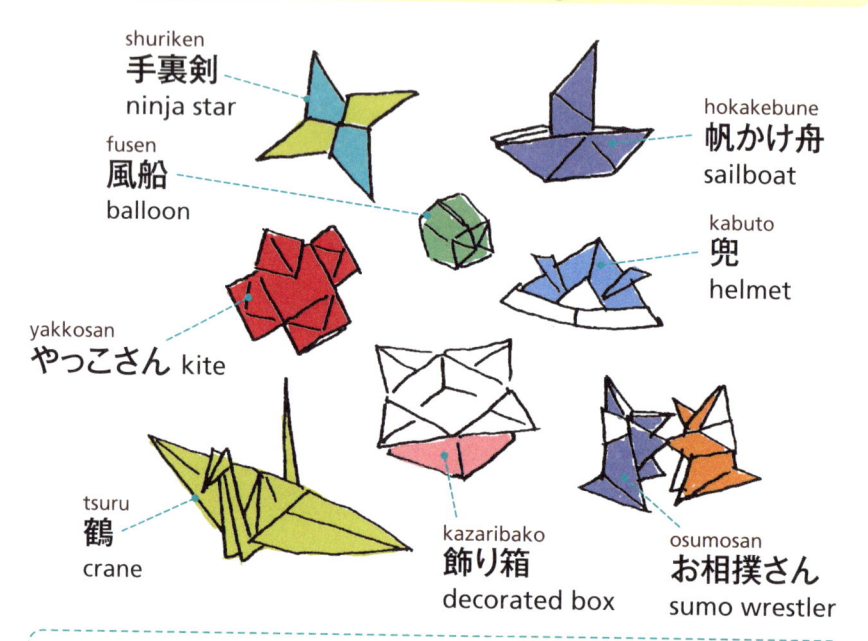

shuriken
手裏剣
ninja star

fusen
風船
balloon

hokakebune
帆かけ舟
sailboat

kabuto
兜
helmet

yakkosan
やっこさん kite

tsuru
鶴
crane

kazaribako
飾り箱
decorated box

osumosan
お相撲さん
sumo wrestler

---

kusudama
くすだま Decorative paper ball

何枚もの折り紙を同じ形に折って、組み合わせて作ります。
A number of identical pieces are made by using multiple sheets of origami and then combining them.

● 鶴の折り方 How to make a crane

1 三角に折り、さらに三角に折ります。

Fold into a triangle, then fold again into a smaller triangle.

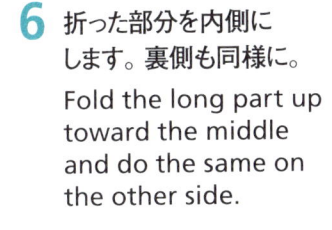

▽

2 袋の部分を開き、四角に折ります。裏側も同様に。

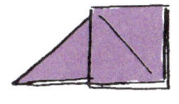

Open the pocket of one half of the triangle and fold to a square. Do the same on the other half.

▽

3 袋の部分を開きます。

Open the pocket.

▽

4 縦に折ります。裏側も同様に。

Fold it length-wise. Do the same on the other side.

▽

5 ひし形の左右の角を内側に折ります。裏側も同様に。

Fold the diamond shaped corners on the left and right sides to the middle. Do the same on the other side.

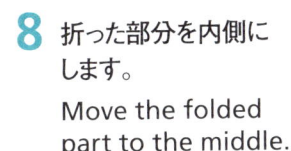

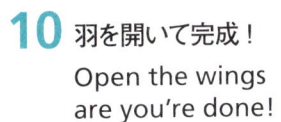

▽

6 折った部分を内側にします。裏側も同様に。

Fold the long part up toward the middle and do the same on the other side.

▽

7 下の部分を上に折ります。裏側も同様に。

Fold the bottom part to the top. Do the same on the other side.

▽

8 折った部分を内側にします。

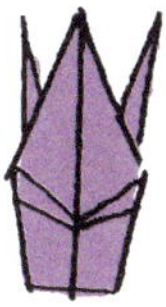

Move the folded part to the middle.

▽

9 片方を折り、頭の形にします。

Fold in one end, making a face.

▽

10 羽を開いて完成！

Open the wings are you're done!

4 日本文化にふれる

Buying souvenirs
＊ Japanese Souvenirs ①
日本のお土産①

yukata
浴衣
informal cotton kimono

jimbei
甚平
light a cotton summer clothing consisting of knee-length shorts and short-sleeved jacket

happi
はっぴ
livery coat

geta
下駄
Japanese wooden sandals

zori
草履
Japanese sandals

kanzashi
かんざし
ornamental hairpin

tenugui
手ぬぐい
towel

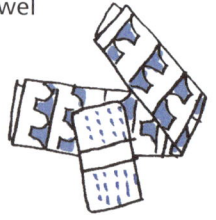

sensu
扇子
folding fan

uchiwa
うちわ
round fan

風呂敷の包み方 How to wrap furoshiki

1 風呂敷の中央に、包むものを置く。
Place the object at the center of the furoshiki.

▽

2 手前の布を、箱の下に折る。
Lift the lower-right corner of the cloth away from you over the box toward the upper-left corner and tuck under the box.

▽

3 奥の布をかぶせる。余った部分は下に折る。
Do the same with the upper-left corner toward you and tuck under the box.

▽

4 布の左右を、中央で真結びする。
Lift both corners and tie with a square knot.

▽

5 完成！　You're done!

5　お土産を買う

---

furoshiki
風呂敷

wrapping cloth

wagasa
和傘

Japanese-style umbrella

chirimen-no-gamaguchi
ちりめんのがまぐち

chirimenpurse made of crape with a metal clasp

111

Buying souvenirs

✳ Japanese Souvenirs ②

日本のお土産②

noren
のれん
short curtain for shop or restaurant

cyochin
ちょうちん
lantern

omen
お面
mask

daruma
だるま
round, red-painted good-luck doll in the shape of Bodhidharma

nihonningyo
日本人形
Japanese doll

nihonto
日本刀
Japanese sword

furin
風鈴
wind-bell

kakejiku
掛け軸
hanging scroll

inro
印籠
pillbox

manekineko
招き猫
cat figure inviting guests and luck

kokeshi
こけし
wooden doll consisting of a cylindrical body with a round head attached

netsuke
根付
miniature buttonlike carving used to hang personal items from a (man's) kimono sash

だるまの目の入れ方
How to paint the eyes in on a daruma.

だるまの左目に黒目を入れ、願いをこめます。
Paint the left eye of daruma in black ink while thinking of a wish that you have.

願いがかなったら、右目に目を入れます。
When your wish is fulfilled, you paint the right eye of daruma in black ink.

願いがかなわなくても、1年を無事にすごせたことを感謝して、右目に目を入れます。
Even if your wish wasn't granted, you should paint the right eye while being thankful that you made it through the year.

5 お土産を買う

113

Buying souvenirs
* Japanese Souvenirs ③
日本のお土産③

kendama
けん玉

cup and ball

koma
こま

piece

tako
たこ

kite

bidama
ビー玉

marble

ohaziki
おはじき

small disc of glass

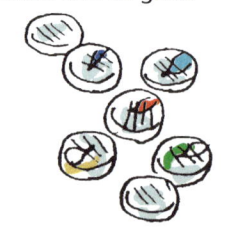

dendendaiko
でんでん太鼓

small drum

kamifusen
紙風船

paper balloon

hagoita
羽子板

battledore

otedama
お手玉

beanbags

darumaotoshi
だるま落とし
daruma game

chiyogami
千代紙
paper with colored figures

taketombo
竹とんぼ
bamboo dragonfly

けん玉の技 Kendama techniques

けん玉の技は、300以上もあるといわれています。
There are more than 300 Kendama techniques.

「大皿」は、けん玉の基本技です。
Ozara is one of the basic kendama techniques.

1 玉をたらす。
Let the kendama hang down.

▷

2 玉を引き上げる。
Toss the ball attached to the stick by a string.

▷

3 玉の下に皿を持っていく。
Catch the ball in the dish.

Traditional customs in Japan

* Annual Events in the Spring

年中行事―春

umemi
● 梅見 2月 Plum blossom viewing February

梅の開花が、早い春の訪れを教えてくれます。
Plum blooming tells us that early spring is coming.

日本各地で、梅まつりが行われます。
Plum blossom festivals are held all over Japan.

hinamatsuri
● ひな祭り 3月3日
Hinamatsuri festival March 3rd

女子の健やかな成長を願います。
People wish for the health and growth of young girls.

ひな人形を飾り、ひしもちや、ひなあられを供えます。
People set up dolls and offer hishimochi and hinaarare.

hanami
● 花見 4月
Cherry blossom viewing April (➡p.76)

日本にはいろいろな花祭りがありますが、
花見といえば桜を表します。
Although there are many flower festivals in Japan, Hanami stands Cherry blossom viewing.

haru-no-ohigan
春のお彼岸 3月中旬頃
The week of Buddhist memorial services centering on the equinox middle of March

お彼岸には、先祖のお墓まいりをします。
春分と秋分をはさみ、1週間行われます。

During the equinox, people visit their ancestors' graves. Equinoctial Week is the week which lasts for one week during the spring and autumn equinoxes.

春にはぼたもち、秋にはおはぎを供えます。

In spring people offer botamochi.
In autumn people offer ohagi.

※「ぼたもち」と「おはぎ」は呼び名が異なるだけで、同じものです。

Botamochi and ohagi are the same sweet, but with different names.

春分=3/21頃
The spring equinox around March 21st

秋分=9/23頃
The autumn equinox around September 23rd

tango-no-sekku
端午の節句 5月5日 Boys' Day May 5th

男の子の健やかな成長を願います。
On Boys' day people wish that each boy in the family will grow up healthy and strong.

こいのぼりや武者人形を飾ります。
They decorate with a carp streamer and a doll warrior.

柏もちや、ちまきを食べる習慣があります。
Eating kashiwamochi and chimaki are customary.

Traditional customs in Japan

✳ Annual Events in the Summer

年中行事—夏

● **七夕** 7月7日 Tanabata July 7th

年に1度、織姫と彦星が天の川で会うことができる日です。

Tanabata is the day on which Vega and Altair can meet once a year.

家庭では7月7日、祭りや行事としては8月7日頃に行われます。

People have Tanabata on July 7th at home. Tanabata festivals and events are held on August 7th.

短冊に願いごとを書いて、笹の葉につるす習慣があります。

It is customary for people to write their wishes on colorful strips of paper and hang them on bamboo branches.

ochugen
● **お中元** 7月1〜15日頃 Midsummer gift July 1st-15th

「中元」とは本来、7月15日のことです。お中元は、この頃に、お世話になっている人に贈り物をする習慣です。

Chugen is originally July 15th. Ochugen is the custom of people giving a gift as a summer greeting to superiors or customers as a token of special thanks for their daily help.

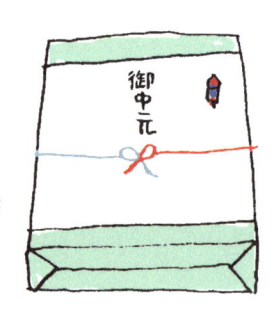

● お盆 7月13〜15日 Obon July 13th-15th

東京では7月13〜15日ですが、全国では月遅れの盆（8月13〜15日）が定着しています。

Obon week is from July 7th to July 15th in Tokyo. It is from July 13th to July 15th (one month later) in most areas of Japan.

お盆の時期には、先祖の魂が帰ってくるといわれています。

Ancestors' spirits return to their families during the Obon period.

家に僧侶を呼んで読経(どきょう)してもらったり、墓参りをします。

People ask a Buddhist monk to come their home to read sutras, or visit graves.

● 盆踊り (bonodori) 8月 Bon festival dance August

全国的には「お盆＝8月」が定着し、盆踊りは8月に行われることが多いです。

People all over Japan think Obon is in August, so the Bon festival dance is usually held in August.

お盆の時期に、浴衣を着て踊り、先祖の供養をします。

During the Obon period, people dance while wearing yukata and hold a memorial service.

6 日本のしきたり

Traditional customs in Japan

✱ Annual Events in the Autumn

年中行事―秋

kiku-no-sekku
菊の節句 9月9日
The chrysanthemum festival September 9th

9月9日は、重陽（菊）の節句。
宮中では祝宴が開かれました。

September 9th is the Chrysanthemum Festival.
People have a celebratory banquet.

otsukimi
お月見 9月中旬頃 Moon viewing middle of September

秋の満月を鑑賞する習慣です。もともとは、秋の収穫を感謝する行事です。

This is the custom of people viewing the full moon. Originally, it was an event during which people express their thanks for the autumn harvest.

すすきを飾り、おだんご、いもを供えて、名月を眺めます。

People decorate Japanese plume grass and offer sweet rice dumplings and potatoes. Then, they view the bright moon.

momijigari
紅葉狩り 10月中旬から
Leaf peeping from the middle of October

落葉樹が鮮やかに色づくと、その美を求めて、散歩や旅に出ます。

When deciduous trees are colored vividly, people go for a walk or travel to see the beautiful colored leaves.

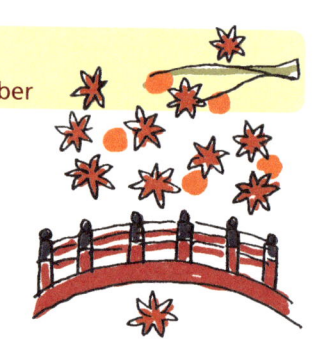

120

budogari　nashimogi
ぶどう狩り、梨もぎ 8月下旬～10月頃
Picking grapes and pears　the end of August to October

園内のぶどうを摘んだり、梨をもいだりして、食べることができます。

You can pick and eat grapes and pears at a plantation.

shichigosan
七五三 11月15日
Festival for 3-year-old boys and girls, 5-year-old boys and 7-year-old girls　November 15th

男の子は5歳、女の子は3歳と7歳に、成長を祝い、神社や寺院にお参りする行事です。

Parents take 5-year-old boys, and 7 and 3-years-old girls to shrines, where they pray for their children's future.

「千歳飴」という、紅白の棒状の飴を食べる習慣があります。

People have a custom of celebrating the day by eating chitoseame.

tori-no-ichi
酉の市 11月 The Bird-day Fair　November

11月の酉の日、日本武尊をまつった神社で行われる祭りです。

The Shinto shrine which enshrines Yamato-Takeruno-Mikoto holds the festival on Tori no hi in November.

酉の市で売られる熊手は、開運、商売繁盛の縁起物です。

Kumade sold at the Bird-day Fair is an auspicious object that brings prosperous business and better luck.

6 日本のしきたり

Traditional customs in Japan

✻ Annual Events in the Winter

年中行事―冬

● **お歳暮** (oseibo) **12月1～15日 Year-end gift** December 1st-15th

お歳暮とは、1年間にお世話に なった人に贈り物をする習慣です。

Oseibo is the custom of people sending a gift to a the person who has assisted them in some way.

● **大掃除** (osoji) **12月28日頃から**
Cleaning up from around December 28th

年末には、掃除をします。

We clean up at the end of a year.

「煤払い(すすはらい)」をし、年神様を迎える 準備という意味もあります。

It means susuharai (the tradition originating from a religious custom in which people cleaned their home altar and rooms) and welcome the god of the New Year.

omisoka
大晦日 12月31日 Omisoka New Year's Eve December 31th

1年の最後の日です。
Omisoka is the last day of the year.

この日に、そばを食べる習慣があります。
There is a custom of eating noodles on this day.

この日の夜から元旦にかけて、多くの寺で、108の煩悩(ぼんのう)を除く意味をこめて、鐘を108回つきます（除夜の鐘）。
Joyano kane means striking a bell one hundred and eight times around 12:00 am on New Year's Eve. This is held in the many temples to remove our 108 desires.

oshogatsu
お正月 1月1〜7日
The New Year January 1st-7th (➡p.124)

nanakusagayu
七草粥 1月7日 Rice porridge with seven herbs January 7th

七草粥を食べて、無病息災を祈ります。
People eat nanakusagayu while praying for their health.

七草粥には、春の七草が入っています。
Nanakusagayu contains seven kinds of spring herbs.

setsubun
節分 2月3日頃 Bean Throwing Night February 3rd

「節分」とはふつう、立春の前日をいい、冬が終わる日のことです。
Setsubun is usually the day before the first day of spring and it is the last day of winter.

「鬼は外、福は内」といいながら、豆をまきます。
People scatter roasted soybeans while saying "In with fortune! Out with evil!".

6 日本のしきたり

123

Traditional customs in Japan

✻ The New Year

お正月

お正月は、年神様が高い山から降りてきて、
子孫の繁栄を見守ってくれるといわれています。

It is said that Toshigami comes down form the high mountain and watches over his descendants' prosperity.

年神様をお迎えするためのさまざまな準備は、年末に行われます。

People prepare for the welcoming of Toshigami at the end of the previous year.

● 注連飾り Shimekazari

門や神棚に注連縄を張って、
神聖な場所であることを示します。

People hang shimekazari over the entrance to their home or their Shinto household altars to show that the place is sacred.

● 門松・松飾り Kadomatsu / Matsukazari

門扉に立てられる、松や竹を使ったお正月の飾りです。ここに年神様が降りるとされています。

Kadomatsu are New Year's decorations with a pair of pines which are placed in front of the gates. It is said that Toshigami comes down on it.

● 雑煮 Zoni

餅が入った汁物です。餅は、昔から、特別な日に食べる食べ物でした。

Zoni is a soup dish which contains rice cakes. People have eaten it on a special days since a long time ago.

● おせち料理 Osechi

縁起ものの料理で、
家族の安全と幸せを祈ります。

It is a dish which brings good luck. People pray for the safety and happiness of their family.

● 初詣 Hatsumode

年が明けてはじめて、神社仏閣に詣でることです。

Hatsumode is the event of visiting a shrine or temple for the first time since the start of a new year.

新しい１年の、健康と幸せを祈ります。

People pray for their health and happiness in the coming year.

Traditional customs in Japan
✱ Shinzenkekkonshiki (Shinto-style Wedding)
神前結婚式

神前結婚式は、神道の神様に結婚を誓う、日本独自の結婚式です。
A shinzenkekkonshiki is a wedding ceremony unique to Japan, in which people pledge their marriage to the Shinto gods.

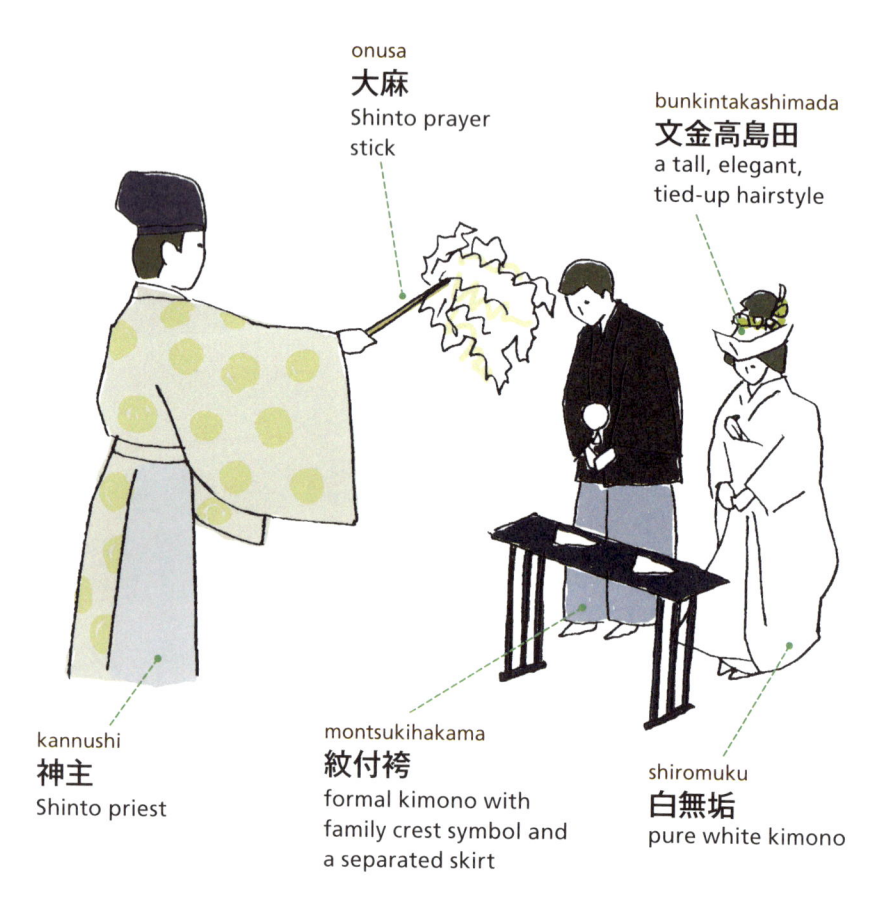

onusa
大麻
Shinto prayer stick

bunkintakashimada
文金高島田
a tall, elegant, tied-up hairstyle

kannushi
神主
Shinto priest

montsukihakama
紋付袴
formal kimono with family crest symbol and a separated skirt

shiromuku
白無垢
pure white kimono

神前結婚で行われること
Rituals in the Shinto-style wedding

sansankudo-no-sakazuki
三三九度の盃

大中小の3つの盃で、新郎新婦が交互にお神酒(みき)を飲みます。

The bride and groom sip sacred sake — three sips from each of three kinds of cups (large, medium, and small).

seishisojo
誓詞奏上

2人で、結婚を誓う言葉を読み上げます。

The bride and groom read their marriage vows.

tamagushihairei
玉串拝礼

2人で、玉串を拝殿に捧げます。

The bride and groom offer a sprig of the sacred sakaki tree in front of a shrine alter.

ご祝儀袋
An envelope containing for a gift money

結婚を祝して、ご祝儀袋にお金を入れて贈ります。

People put money in an envelope and give it as a wedding gift.

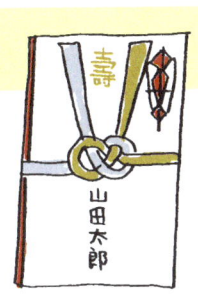

寿
山田太郎

Traditional customs in Japan
✱ Ososhiki Funerals
お葬式

日本では、キリスト教徒を除いて、葬式の多くが仏式で行われます。
Most of the funeral ceremonies in Japan are observed as Buddhist ritual funeral services, except for Christian funerals.

葬儀（告別式）の前の晩には、通夜が行われます。
A tsuya is a ritual held throughout the night before the day of the funeral.

通夜・葬儀では、僧侶がお経を上げるなか、参列者が1人ずつお焼香をして、死者の冥福を祈ります。
During the tsuya and funeral service, people burn incense and pray for the dead person's soul to rest in peace while a Buddhist monk reads sutras.

通夜・葬儀から帰宅したら、家に入る前に身体に塩をかけて身を清めます。
When you come back home from tsuya and the funeral service, you should sprinkle salt on your body before entering the house.

● 葬儀の服装
Clothing for funeral service

※通夜の服装は、正式の喪服でなくてもかまいません。

You can also go to a tsuya with informal black clothing.

● お香典
Okoden condolence money for a funeral

線香などの代わりに、死者の霊前に供える
ために、お金を包み、受付で手渡します。

You should hand over your condolence money
in exchange for incense at the reception.

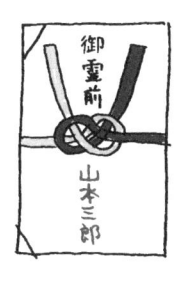

「このたびはご愁傷様です」
I share your pain.

● お焼香の仕方 How to burn incense

1 遺族と僧侶に一礼、遺影に一礼して手を合わせます。

You should bow to the surviving members of
the family and to the Buddhist monk. Then,
you bow to a portrait of a deceased person
and put your hands together.

▽

2 右手の指先でお香をつまみ、目の高さまで上げます。

Hold the incense level with your forehead.

▽

3 お香を香炉にくべます。

Put the incense in the incense burner.

▽

4 再び手を合わせて、一礼します。

Put your hands together again and bow once.

※お焼香の回数は、1〜3回。宗派によって異なります。
The number of times you should burn the incense is one to
three times, depending on the sect.

6 日本のしきたり

Hospitality English Professional

✳ Greetings
挨拶をする

● 日常の挨拶 Everyday greetings

おはようございます。
Good morning.

こんにちは。
Good afternoon.

こんばんは。
Good evening.

行ってきます。
I'm leaving.

行ってらっしゃい。
Have a nice day.

ただいま。
I'm home.

お帰りなさい。
Welcome home.

● ご機嫌うかがい Asking about

いかがおすごしですか?
How are you doing?

いかがですか?
How's everything?
How's everything going?

元気です。
I'm fine.
I'm good.
I'm doing well. Thank you.

まあまあです。
Not too bad.

元気にしていましたか?
How have you been?

元気でしたよ。あなたはどうですか?
I've been great. And you?

久しぶりですね。
Long time no see.
It's been quite a while.

いいお天気ですね。
It's a beautiful day.

● 別れの挨拶 Greeting when leaving

さようなら。
Good bye.

またね。
See you.

会えてよかったです。
It was nice meeting you.

お話しできて、とても楽しかったです。
I had a great time talking with you.

ご一緒できて、すばらしい一日でした。
I had a wonderful time with you today.

連絡を取り合いましょうね。
Let's keep in touch.

Hospitality English Professional

✳ Meeting Someone
知り合う

● 初対面の挨拶 Greeting when meeting for the first time

はじめまして。
Nice to see you.
Good to see you.

こちらこそ、よろしくお願いします。
Nice to meet you too.

やっと会えてうれしいです。
It's so nice to finally meet you.

お目にかかれて光栄です。
It's a pleasure to meet you.

お話しできて楽しかったです。
It was nice talking to you.

私たち、まだお目にかかってなかったですね。
I don't believe we've met before.

● 質問する When you ask someone a question

どこから来たのですか?
Where do you come from?

いつ日本に来たのですか?
When did you come to Japan?

どのくらいいるのですか?
How long are you going to stay ?

日本は初めてですか?
Is this your first visit to Japan?

何のために、日本に来たのですか?
What made you come to Japan?

日本はどうですか?
How do you find Japan?

どんなところに行きましたか?
Where have you been in Japan?

個人的な質問をしてもいいですか?
Do you mind if I ask you a personal question?

いつ会えますか?
When can we meet?

名前を聞いてもいいですか?
May I have your name, please?

メールアドレスを聞いてもいいですか?
If you don't mind, could I have your e-mail address?

聞き取れないとき When you can't understand what she (or he or they) said

もう少しゆっくり話してください。
Could you speak more slowly?

もう一度お願いします。
Could you say that again?

ちょっと待ってください。
Could you wait for a moment?

ここに書いてください。
Please write down here.

日本語はわかりますか?
Do you understand Japanese?

Hospitality English Professional

✳ Introducing Yourself
自己紹介をする

● 名前 Name

タクと呼んでください。
Please call me Taku.

タクでいいですよ。
You can call me Taku.

● 住まい・出身 Residence and hometown

どこに住んでいますか?
Where do you live?

東京に住んでいます。
I live in Tokyo.

東京の立川市に住んでいます。
I'm living in Tachikawa, Tokyo.

山形出身です。
I'm from Yamagata.

京都生まれですが、東京育ちです。
I was born in Kyoto but I grew up in Tokyo.

東京出身ですが、大阪で暮らしたこともあります。
I'm from Tokyo but I've lived in Osaka, too.

● 趣味 Hobbies

趣味は何ですか?
What is your hobby?
What do you like to do in your free time?

趣味はゴルフです。
My hobby is playing golf.

料理が好きです。
I like cooking.

旅行が大好きです。
I love traveling.

アウトドアが好きです。
I love spending time outdoors.

● 仕事 Job

どんな仕事をしていますか?
What line of work are you in?
What do you do for a living?

販売員をしています。
I'm a shop clerk.

GWEで働いています。
I work for GWE.

IT関連の仕事をしています。
I work in IT.

ウェブデザイナーです。
I'm a web designer.

● その他 Etc.

ひとり暮らしですが、犬を2匹飼っています。
I live by myself, but I have two dogs.
I'm living alone, but I have two dogs.

うちは大家族です。
I have a big family.

Hospitality English Professional

✱ Showing Someone the Way ①
道案内をする①

● 道案内をする Showing a person the way to……

ここへは、どうやって行けばいいですか?
How can I get to this place?

東京駅はどこですか?
Do you know where I can find Tokyo station?

ここからいちばん近い駅はどこですか?
Where is the nearest train station?

この道をまっすぐ行ってください。
Go down this street.

2ブロックまっすぐ進んでください。
Go straight for two blocks.

角にあるホテルが見えるまで、まっすぐ行ってください
Go straight on this street until you see a hotel.

信号を右に曲がってください。
Turn right at the traffic light.

郵便局をすぎて、右に曲がってください。
Go past the post office and turn right.

書店を通りすぎてください。
Go past the bookstore.

反対側の道に行ってください。
Cross the street.

橋の下をくぐってください。
Go under the bridge.

● 場所を示す Indicating the location

銀座通りにあります。
It's on Ginza street.

駅の近くにあります。
It's near the station.
It's just a ten-minute walk.

コンビニの隣にあります。
It's next to the convenience store.

交番の向かいにあります。
It's opposite the police box.

コンビニは、この道を5ブロックほど行ったGMスーパーの前にあります。
There is a convenience store about five blocks this way and it's in front of the GM supermarket.

● 距離を伝える Telling someone which way to go

だいたい徒歩10分くらいで着きます。
It takes about 10 minutes on foot.

ここからそんなに遠くないです。
It's not that far from here.

すぐそこですよ。
It's quite close.

歩くには遠いです。
It's a long way to walk.

かなり遠いですよ。
It's too far.

かなり遠いので、バスに乗ったほうがいいですよ。
It's pretty far from here, so you'd better take a bus.

Hospitality English Professional

✳ Showing Someone the Way ②
道案内をする②

● 鉄道の案内をする Giving information about a train

この電車は、新宿に行きますか？
Does this train take me to Shinjuku?

はい。行きますよ。
Yes, it does.

いいえ。行きません。山手線に乗り換えてください。
No, it doesn't. You should transfer to the Yamamote line.

次の駅で中央線に乗り換えてください。
Change to the Chuo line at the next stop.

渋谷まであと何駅ですか？
How many stops is Shibuya station form here?

ここから6駅です。
It's six from here.

地下鉄のほうがいいですよ。
The subway would be better.

羽田空港に行きたいのですが。
I'd like to go to the Haneda Airport.

東京駅で山手線に乗って品川方面へ行き、浜松町で降りてください。
Take the Yamanote line for Shinagawa station and get off at Hamamatsucho.

● 交通手段を選ぶ Choosing transportation

もっとも早いのは電車です。
The fastest way is to take a train.

もっともいいのはバスです。
The best way is to take a bus.

タクシーを拾いましょうか?
Shall I get a taxi for you?

● わかりません I don't know.

ごめんなさい。わかりません。駅員に聞いてください。
I'm sorry. I don't know. Please ask a station attendants.

誰かほかの人に聞いてもらえますか?
Could you ask someone else?

この場所にはくわしくないんです。
I'm a stranger here. I'm not from here.

● 道案内で使う単語 Words for showing someone the way

角 corner
交差点 cross road
横断歩道 crossing
歩道橋 footbridge
看板 sign
階段 stairs
信号 traffic light
地下道 underpass

まっすぐ行く go straight
通りすぎる go past
右へ曲がる turn right
左へ曲がる turn left
〜の隣 next to〜

Hospitality English Professional

✳ Offering Assistance

手伝いを申し出る

● 声かけをする Addressing a person

お手伝いしましょうか?
Do you need some help?

何かお探しですか?
May I help you find something?
Are you looking for something?

切符を買うのを、手伝いましょうか?
Do you need help buying a ticket?

● 案内を申し出る
Offering to give someone a tour of a place

道に迷っています。
I'm lost.

一緒に行きましょうか?
Shall I go with you?

地図を書きましょうか?
Shall I draw you a map?

案内しますので、ついて来てください。
Let me take you there. Follow me, please.
I'll show you the way. Follow me, please.

● 写真を撮る Taking pictures

写真を撮ってあげましょうか？
Shall I take your photo?

よかったら写真をお撮りしましょうか？
I can take your photo if you like.
Shall I take a picture for you?
Would you like me to take your picture?

いいですか？　はい、チーズ！
Are you ready? Say Cheese!

● その他 Etc.

ここでは電話は使えません。
You can't use your phone here.

ここにはWi-fiがありますよ。
There is Wi-fi here.

セットアップを手伝いましょうか？
I'll help you set it up.

警察に通報したほうがいいですよ。
You should call the police.

警察はあっちです。
The police station is over there.

Hospitality English Professional

✳ Calling

電話をする

● 電話を受ける Receiving someone's call

どちら様ですか?

Who's calling, please?
May I have your name, please?

スペルを教えてもらえますか?

How do you spell your name?
May I have the spelling, please?
Could you spell your name for me?

誰におかけですか?

Who(m) would you like to speak to?

かけ間違いではないですか?

I'm afraid you have the wrong number.

お待ちください。

Hold on, please.
Hold the line, please.
Just a moment, please.

お待たせしました。

Thank you for waiting.
Sorry to keep you waiting.

● 電話をかける Calling someone

もしもし、山田です。

Hello, this is Yamada speaking.

青山はるかですが、ホワイトさんはいますか?

Hello. This is Haruka Aoyama. May I speak to Mr. White, please?

いつ戻りますか?
Do you know when she will be back?

電話番号を間違えました。ごめんなさい。
I must have the wrong number. I'm sorry.

● 相手が不在のとき
When he (or she or they) is(are) not available

あとで、かけなおします。
I'll call him back later.

伝言をお願いできますか?
Can I leave a message?

鈴木から電話があったと伝えてもらえますか?
Could you please tell him that Suzuki called?

彼女に折り返し電話をくれるように、伝えてもらえますか?
Could you tell her to call me back?

● ビジネスの場で In business situations

申し訳ありませんが、彼女はいま、別の電話に出ております。
I'm sorry, but she is on another line right now.

申し訳ありませんが、ただいま会議中です。
I'm sorry, but he is in a meeting right now.

何時に戻るかわからないのですが。
I'm not sure when he will be back.

今日は戻らない予定になっています。
She won't be back today.

ご伝言はありますか?
Would you like to leave a message?
Can I take your message?

折り返し電話をさせましょうか?
Shall I have her call you back?

Hospitality English Professional

* Caring about Someone

気遣う

● 健康を気遣う Caring about someone's health

お疲れですか?
Are you tired?

休憩しましょうか?
Do you need a break?

疲れていないといいのですが。
I hope you aren't tired.

歩くことは大丈夫ですか?
Do you mind walking?

● 体調を気遣う Caring about someone's fatigue

大丈夫ですか?
Are you OK?

気分はどうですか?
How are you feeling?

横になりますか?
Would you like to lie down?

何か食べたほうがいいですよ。
You should eat something.

何か私にできることはありますか?
Is there anything I can do for you?

お医者さんに行ったほうがいいです。
You should go see a doctor.

病院へ行かなくてはなりません。
I need to go to the hospital.

● 気遣い Caring

こちらの席に座ってください（電車で席を譲る）。
Please have this seat here.

お待たせしてごめんなさい。
I'm sorry to kept you waiting.

大丈夫ですよ。急がないでください。
It's OK. Don't rush.

いつが都合がいいですか？
When would be convenient for you?

あなたの日本語はとても上手です。
Your Japanese is very good.

あなたの気持ち、わかります。
I know where you 're coming from.

Hospitality English Professional

✻ Welcoming Someone, Asking Someone Something, Chiming in
出迎え・お願い・あいづち

● 出迎える Welcoming someone

飛行機では眠れましたか?
Did you get some sleep on the plane?

日本に来てくれて、本当にうれしいです。
I'm really happy that you are here.

あなたに会えるのを、楽しみにしていました。
I've been looking forward to seeing you.

明日は何がしたいですか?
What would you like to do tomorrow?

日本にいる間に、何か特に見たい場所はありますか?
Is there anywhere in particular that you'd like to see while you're here in Japan?

ささやかな贈り物です。
Here is a little something for you.

● お願いする Asking someone something

お願いがあります。
Would you do me a favor?

手伝ってくれますか?
Could you help me, please?

いいですよ。
Sure.

ドアを閉めてくれますか?
Would you please close the door?

● あいづちを打つ Chiming in

確かに。
I'm sure.

確かではありません。
I'm not sure.

わかっています。
I know.

わかります。
I see.
I understand.

本当ですか?
Really?

もちろんです。
OF course.
Sure.

問題ありません。
No problem.

その通りです。
That's right.

たぶん。
Maybe.

そう思います。
I think so.

Hospitality English Professional

✳ Having a Meal

食事をする

● 食事をする Having a meal

いただきます。
Let's eat.

乾杯！
Cheers!

おいしいです。
It tastes good.
It tastes delicious.

これは苦手です。残してもいいですか？
I can't handle it. Could I leave the rest of it?

ごちそうさまでした。
That was a delicious meal!
I enjoyed the meal very much.

● お店で At a restaurant

注文をお願いします。
I'd like to order.

これはどんな料理ですか？
What kind of dish is this?

おすすめは何ですか。
What do you recommend?

ビールをもう1杯ください。
Could you give me another glass of beer?

日本酒はありますか？
Do you have Japanese-sake?

お勘定をお願いします。
May we have the check, please?

● 食事をふるまう To treat someone to a meal

食べ物では、何が好きですか？
What kind of food do you like?

食べられないものはありますか？
Is there anything you can't eat?

日本にいる間に、何か食べたいものはありますか？
Is there anything you'd like to eat while you are in Japan?

多すぎたら残してくださいね。
If it's too much to eat, you may leave it.

おかわりはいかがですか？
Would you like more?

コーヒーと紅茶、どちらがいいですか？
Which would you like, coffee or tea?

コーヒーより、紅茶のほうが好きです。
I prefer tea to coffee.

● 提案する Making a proposal

デパ地下に行くといいですよ。
I recommend that you go to Depachika.

お茶席に興味はありますか？
Are you interested in a tea ceremony?

Hospitality English Professional

✳ Advice for Buying Souvenirs

お土産のアドバイス

● お土産のアドバイス Advice for buying souvenirs

浅草や鎌倉には、土産物屋がたくさんあります。
There are many gift shops in Asakusa and Kamakura.

伝統的なものと現代的なもの、どちらがいいですか?
Which would you like, something traditionally Japanese or something contemporary?

伝統的なふろしきはどうですか?
How about some traditional furoshiki?

買い物には、銀座がおすすめですよ。
I recommend Ginza for shopping.

● お店で At the shop

いらっしゃいませ
Welcome to our shop.

おすすめのお土産は何ですか?
What do you recommend for a souvenir?

これは人気があります。
This is popular.

これを3つください。
I'll take three of these.

プレゼント用に包んでください。
Please gift-wrap it.

Hospitality English Professional

✽ Emergencies

緊急事態

● 緊急事態 Emergency

助けて！
Help!

緊急事態です！
It's an emergency!

泥棒！
Robber!
Thief!

泥棒を捕まえて！
Please catch the thief!

警察に電話して！
Call the police, please.

救急車を呼んで！
Call the ambulance.

財布をなくしました。
I've lost my wallet.

パスポートをなくしました。
I lost my passport.

すぐに私のカードを無効にしてください。
Could you cancel my credit cards immediately?

staff

イラスト／ひらいみも
ブックデザイン／永瀬優子、武田理沙（ごぼうデザイン事務所）
編集協力／Take One

本書に関する質問は、以下の質問係まで、郵便または電子メールにてお願いいたします。
電話によるお問い合わせ、また本書の範囲を超えるご質問等にはお答えできません。
あらかじめご了承ください。

〈読者質問係〉
〒101-8405　東京都千代田区三崎町2-18-11
二見書房
『イラストで解る！英語で日本のしきたりと文化を伝える本』質問係
電子メール　info@futami.co.jp

イラストで解る！
英語で日本のしきたりと文化を伝える本

著者　荒井弥栄（あらいやえ）

発行　株式会社二見書房
　　　東京都千代田区三崎町 2-18-11
　　　電話　03（3515）2311［営業］
　　　　　　03（3515）2314［編集］
　　　振替　00170-4-2639

印刷　株式会社堀内印刷所

製本　株式会社村上製本所

落丁・乱丁がありました場合は、お取り替えします。
定価はカバーに表示してあります。

©Yae Arai, 2016, Printed in Japan
ISBN978-4-576-16111-2
http://www.futami.co.jp